The Lived International

Creative Interventions in Global Politics

Series Editors: Shine Choi, Cristina Masters, Swati Parashar, and Marysia Zalewski

The landscape of contemporary global politics is complex and oftentimes violent. Yet the urgency to provide solutions or immediate practical actions to this violence oftentimes leads to inadequate knowledge. This is despite the abundance of theoretical, conceptual, and methodological tools available—much of this produced through conventional academic disciplines, notably international relations, political theory, and philosophy. But the constraints imposed on these traditional disciplines profoundly limit their ability to incorporate and make effective use of more creative and innovative methodologies found in other disciplines and genres. This series provides a unique opportunity to offer creative intellectual space to work with an eclectic and rich range of disciplines and approaches, including performative methodologies, storytelling, narrative and autoethnography, embodied research methodologies, participant research, visual and film methodologies, and arts-based methodologies.

Titles in the Series

The Lived International

A Life in International Relations

Stephen Chan

ROWMAN & LITTLEFIELD
Lanham • Boulder • New York • London

Published by Rowman & Littlefield
An imprint of The Rowman & Littlefield Publishing Group, Inc.
4501 Forbes Boulevard, Suite 200, Lanham, Maryland 20706
www.rowman.com

86-90 Paul Street, London EC2A 4NE, United Kingdom

British Library Cataloguing in Publication Information Available

Library of Congress Cataloging-in-Publication Data

Names: Chan, Stephen, 1949– author.
Title: The lived international: a life in international relations / Stephen Chan.
Description: Lanham: Rowman & Littlefield, [2022] | Series: Creative interventions in global politics | Includes bibliographical references and index. | Summary: "This book proposes that a life of praxis, living international relations, yields more insights than a life of theory alone"—Provided by publisher.
Identifiers: LCCN 2021055954 (print) | LCCN 2021055955 (ebook) | ISBN 9781538164976 (cloth) | ISBN 9781538164990 (paperback) | ISBN 9781538164983 (epub)
Subjects: LCSH: Chan, Stephen, 1949– | International relations—Philosophy. | International relations specialists—Biography. | International relations—Poetry.
Classification: LCC JZ1305.C429 2022 (print) | LCC JZ1305 (ebook) | DDC 327.101—dc23/eng/20220106
LC record available at https://lccn.loc.gov/2021055954
LC ebook record available at https://lccn.loc.gov/2021055955

Contents

Contents

Preface

This is a book I have resisted writing for many years. However, having now entered my seventies, and having decided in my sixties to desist from going to war zones, perhaps enough tumult in my life has settled for some critical reflection to take place. I have built this book around some key periods of my life that were also marked by creative interventions (i.e., poems). Many of the poems in this book were previously published, some anthologised, so it is as a recognised poet, especially in New Zealand literary history, that I compose a book of this sort.[1]

There have been many requests to write something like this. I had earlier hoped my brief contribution to Naeem Inayatullah's volume would satisfy such requests.[2] But, ten years later, the requests have continued. And the reason for this is because it was clear I was allergic to armchairs and had wandered the world all my life seeking to live the international and, having first lived it, then think it. This has not simply been a case of bearing witness. It has been about helping nations emerge from war, building government ministries in new states and states recovering from trauma, immersing myself in slums, resolving conflict on the sites of conflict, and taking part in high negotiations. All of this has been without seeking to become a senior international official—although I was, when young, a middling such official and, because young and middling enough to be expendable, sent off to accomplish some interestingly difficult things. Since my mid-thirties, all my work has been as a private citizen, beholden to no one except my sense of necessity. To speak truth to power is not a long-distance conversation with health and safety regulations.

But I am not as rigorous as the late Susan Sontag who, having emerged alive from the siege of Sarajevo, issued almost an edict that, if you have never been there, never suffered as those there suffer, you may not speak.[3] Of course you should speak. But my academic discipline of international relations does, in my view, require many more people to speak from direct confrontation with power and its misuses. To theorise the pain of the world, for instance, reduces the task to that of a clinician if at least some of that pain has not been even briefly shared or directly observed.

Not all of that pain is expressible academically and certainly not logically, not even with panoplies of psychoanalytic diagnoses. Some of it is too complex even for poetry. In the case of the terror and pain in Uganda in the wake of Amin, clear through to the atrocious rebellion of Joseph Kony, I was only able to outline some of this complexity in an experimental novel.[4] The reader of this current book will at least be spared my novels, but the poems will be there as creations that help interpret what I myself have often felt otherwise inexpressible and unable to be interpreted by ordinary means. They relate a personal effort to think as far as I can. My inflected position is that academic thought needs to be augmented by other thought and, even then, we might be able only to feel tentatively the contours of the inexpressible.

As a young schoolboy I tried to read Wittgenstein's *Tractatus*. Of course it was a disaster in terms of understanding it. But his final proposition, number 7, struck home. That which cannot be expressed in words should be passed over in silence. I reinterpreted that in two ways: what cannot be expressed with logic might be expressed in poetry; what is passed over in silence may mean the end of words, but it is not the end of silent action. I have tried to write the international. When, even with poetry that failed, I have continued to act it. If I had finally found the bullet with my name on it, finally fallen out of the sky as my light aircraft crashed, finally succumbed to the violent convulsions of malaria, I would at least have lived the international.

Stephen Chan
London 2020

NOTES

1. See the definitive anthology of New Zealand poetry from my period of publishing in that country: Alan Brunton, Murray Edmond, & Michele Leggott (eds.), *Big Smoke: New Zealand Poems 1960–1975*, Auckland: Auckland University Press, 2000, pp 218–222. And my most critically received book of poetry from that era: Stephen Chan, *Arden's Summer*, Christchurch: Pegasus, 1975. See D. S. Long, "Chinese Poetry in New Zealand," *Canta*, 6 September 1971, in which I am treated as the nation's primary and pioneering Chinese poet; a critical position more recently expressed by Vaughn Rapatahana in the University of Pennsylvania journal, *Jacket 2*: "He must be considered the precursor Kiwi-Asian poet." http://jacket2.org/commentary/kiwi-asian-poetry, 29 September 2015.

2. Stephen Chan, "Accidental Scholarship and the Myth of Objectivity," in Naeem Inayatullah (ed.), *Autobiographical International Relations: I, IR*, London: Routledge, 2011.

3. She made this edict in 1997 to the French journal *La Regle du Jeu*, and it is included in Susan Sontag, *Where the Stress Falls*, London: Jonathan Cape, 2002, p 298. See also Benjamin Moser, *Sontag: Her Life*, London: Allen Lane, 2019, chapters 34–36. Stephen Chan, "The Pain of Susan Sontag," *Global Society*, 24:3, 2010, pp 369–380.

4. Stephen Chan, *Joseph Kony and the Titans of Zagreb*, London: Nth Position, 2012.

Chapter 1

Receiving the International

International relations began as an academic discipline in response to the carnage of modern war. Welsh millionaire David Davies, appalled by the slaughter of World War I but impressed by the open diplomacy proposed by Woodrow Wilson, endowed in 1919 the first chair in the subject at Aberystwyth.[1] But those two animations from the start established a dualism in the discipline: a study of war and the reality of its political condition, and the search for peace as an ideal condition. The two schools, variously named realism and behaviouralist, one the one side, idealism, pluralism, and utopianism, on the other, were in due course joined by a third, structuralism, borrowed from neo-Marxist theories of development in which the world was one of accumulations directed by a metropolitan centre through an international cascade of class-bound elites. The three schools did not much talk to one another, so much so that Michael Banks described them as three paradigms,[2] borrowing from Thomas Kuhn's idea of self-reinforcing knowledge that could not be reformed but only overthrown.[3] As paradigms the three schools were basically incommensurable, and the division into paradigms was taken up by editors as a ready means for depicting the discipline. A book only needed to have three parts and the discipline was covered.[4] Those who did not wish to accommodate structuralism needed to discourse on only two.[5] And, even with two, there were internal divisions as to whether their study was best served by quantitative or qualitative means.[6] And it was perfectly possible to write a classic text that emphasised only one.[7]

   Much later, in the late 1980s, the discipline began to adopt a fourth school, one of norms and critical theory—a movement that occurred much later than in political philosophy, drawn from the Frankfurt School of World War II, which, in the wake of Hitler's depredations in Europe, and his desecration of Enlightenment ethics, sought a modern speaking of truth to power by way of thought refracted through the experience of tragedy.[8] Even so, critical theory soon divided itself into two, with French as well as German schools, the former with a tinge of postmodernism but concentrated for the most part on the

1

structure of the discursive world proposed by Foucault. What was truth and how to know one was speaking truth, whether to power or not, became a pre-occupation—so that international relations had completed a circle, from its origin in wartime power, to a speaking of truth that interrogated itself while accepting power almost as a background given. By 1990, the discipline was certainly vibrant, and a mess.

This was the state of the discipline in the United Kingdom when I accepted a position at the University of Kent. Into this discipline, not long after several years in Africa, and shortly before a feminist IR joined the ranks[9]—a first sign of "difference"—I arrived confounded by what I discovered. The discipline contained much with which I agreed—but had nevertheless reified itself from the world of struggle and desire I had just experienced. A reification not quite to abstraction, but with an ambition to stretch itself, divisions and all, as cara-pace over a world that was messy enough not to fit any paradigm or school, enigmatic enough not to be diagnosed in terms of European norms, "illogi-cal" enough not to be amenable to scientific investigation, confusing enough where elites were leaders of liberation as well as exploiters, and aspirational enough to defy any assumption that development arose from an original intel-lectual backwardness. I was grateful for employment—I had given away all my money in Africa—and I was affronted.

I had previously taught at the University of Zambia for two years, 1983–1985, after I had resigned my post as an international civil servant. I had then completed a month-long mission seeking to reconstruct ministerial provision in the chaos and infrastructural meltdown that Amin had left behind in Uganda. I traveled throughout the country, often steering by compass as roads had disappeared, and saw sufficient legacies of terror that I thought no international agency could address. Roads and buildings could in due course be repaired. Trauma and dislocation would remain as spirits to haunt the land for years. So I tendered my resignation as an international official, with misgiving, but I had decided in the spirit-driven Ruwenzori Mountains, what Speke and Burton had called the Mountains of the Moon, that writing honestly might be better than acting partially. This mission to Uganda was in fact my second effort to reach the country. The first came in 1980 when I was shortlisted as the UK-designated lorry driver in an early plan by the UNHCR to distribute emergency food in the starving country. Each driver had to come from a different country. I lied that I had a heavy vehicles licence. Completely at odds with the prevailing UN playbook, we were to drive in any direction, wherever we could—in fact, for lorries, that turned out to be not very far, given the lack of roads and petrol depots—and just give the food to any hungry village we came across. At the last minute, the UN returned to form and decided to plan and bureaucratise each step, abandoning wild and random humanitarianism. Seriously delayed humanitarianism resulted.

But, yes, Uganda was for these reasons why I decided to enter academic life. In any case, while in the Ruwenzori Mountains, I found myself involved in settling a small civil war. That was totally unscripted. I never told my superiors about that. It was off-mission. So I sought the freedom to be responsive to things that were not meant to be. And I never told my superiors that, in fact, rogue armies still roamed the country, and that doing what my mission entailed necessitated some serious navigation, negotiation, and staring down adult and child soldiers who were pointing AK47s at me from a metre away. If my superiors had known the true state of the country I would never have been sent. But I decided I wished also for the freedom to take risks. I wrote a poem about this freedom, and its conditionalities, and it features my driver, here named Moabite, from the nation not chosen by God and who were shunned by the Israelites—for no other government driver would accept the assignment to drive me where I wanted to go. He was the outcast in the drivers' pool.[10]

"Moabite and the Mountains of the Moon"

He called him Moabite
for Moabites were a cursed race.
Even so, he'd defended him
when, surrounded by strongarmers
from God knows which army,
whips raised to beat the wizened driver,
he pushed his way through,
passes of immunity in hand,
led the tiny black man off.

For Moabite was the only driver,
bagman, thief, drunkard, living beyond
life's nine chances,
opposer of conditionality,
squanderer of life on his own sad terms,
assigned to him one day
in Kampala's summer heat,
all others knowing the journey was perilous.

Ah, Moabite,
deceitful volunteer,
brought back from record suspensions
immediately traded in petrol tank,
tyres and dashboard fuses,
fitted his worn replacements,
drank the profits in one afternoon.

We are heading, bwana, beyond the
invasion route, beyond the Tanzanian march,
towards Zaire, into the Mountains of the Moon;
don't be concerned with leaking petrol,
every two kilometres I'll stop,
wipe stolen soap across the holes;
the smooth as pebble tyres are under a spell
as powerful as German tread;
it will not rain at night,
the single dashboard fuse need never
anchor wiper blades and headlights
simultaneously.
I, your faithful Moabite, will carry you safe.

True to his word he hoarded his soap,
never washing, he plugged his petrol leaks.
No tyres blew.
At nights, when rains came down,
he'd stare through the torrent,
regarded not the road
but trees overhead,
explained his positioning of the headlights
—straight up bwana—
with trees on either side
we rode the ribbon through,
a centre-line for Moabite.

Ah, but how, I'd ask, will you fake it
in those Mountains of the Moon?
Where mountain wall will rise like
a tablet of commandment,
sinner's sheer drop on the other side.
When winds will howl and
in night's dark domain
distant snow-capped peaks
will tempt you to leap black
invisible canyons,
fly like God's chosen cherub,
laughed at by demons come to requisition
the broken landrover and your broken life.

In the Mountains of the Moon
Moabite sang, hands intermittently steering,
grasping bottles,
feet pushing pedals,

clutching to a beat far in his head.
Oh, bwana, sleep,
dream of your far lands,
these many night-time hours
your mission's in Moabite's tender hands,
will see you safe, bwana,
will see you whole,
but sleep, please dream,
pretty ones at your home.

Who knows what spells Moabite chanted,
what promises he made the mountains,
what codewords he gave the soldiers
seeking highway toll.

But debouched one green and freezing morning
into a valley of sheep, banana trees,
quotations from Yeats
on schoolroom's broken wall.
I've brought you to your destination,
to the pinpricks on the maps,
I, the faithful Moabite,
the dissolute, disillusioned Moabite,
the dregs of the car-pool drivers,
and have come, myself, to childhood home,
to the Mountains of the Moon,
an individual rule in African sun's hot dominion.
On high peaks I sang,
oh, one thousand cantos
for lost loves long ago
for, bwana, I also loved
and do you think
now that I have brought you to the source
of my wizened alchemy
you will not one day
howl in mountains
worship Moon's cool light,
and, some princeling's hired dreg,
slouch homewards
like a man
outrunning his curse
and make a claim, as I do now,
being disused
to be paid off
and dismissed?

Afterward, I spent a few months as a Visiting Fellow at Queen Elizabeth House, Oxford. Then the University of Zambia offered me a post in international relations. But, when I took up the post I found that the most recent books in the library on the subject were twenty years old. Zambia too was economically destitute. Even paper and ink were rationed at the university— so I stole a vast stock of these items and bribed the university's gestetner operator to print off copies of each of my lectures. I laboriously typed each one as if it were a fully written chapter in a text book, again on stolen stencils, and distributed these week by week to my students. It was a text book written entirely from memory of an older form of the discipline, made as modern as possible by my use of recent case examples. And it was written to be meaningful to an African audience. The junior minister of foreign affairs, deputy ambassadors, and army colonels came to my lectures. It was the only course of its sort in the free countries of Southern Africa. In 1985, as the second year of my lecturing began, I returned to my office one day to find a young blond man waiting at my door. "Hello, I'm from Macmillan in the United Kingdom. We've heard about your lectures. We want to offer you a contract." Of course it doesn't happen like that now. I went back to Queen Elizabeth House and added footnotes to the manuscript. The World Bank purchased several thousand copies of the published book for distribution to African universities and students.[11] It was because of that, and my experience as an international civil servant, that the University of Kent hired me. But I came back to a discipline that was not as I remembered it when writing the book. No one was writing international relations with Africa in mind, then not even with China in mind, except as an object in Western thought, theory, and strategy. As I said, I was affronted.

I sought to absorb as much as possible of what had developed. I was able to teach courses on African politics and international organization, and I read as deeply as I could on each of the three paradigms. The structuralist approach to *dependencia* was familiar enough. Before I had gone to live in Africa, I was in the office next door to the secretariat of the Brandt Commission as they prepared what became a valiant report that sought a new international economic order.[12] Hans Singer and Dudley Seers, the two founders of the Sussex Institute of Development Studies, had taken a kind interest in the background papers I had prepared for conferences sponsored by my institution. I was not convinced, however, that it could be devolved to a question of class and the global relations of class. Liberal pluralism I understood: I had worked in this field. Power I saw in the spectacularly hot nature of the Cold War in Africa as described by Fred Halliday.[13] And, in terms of the developing interest in continental philosophy, I was at least familiar with the writings of the generation before Foucault, that of Sartre and Beauvoir. What I missed in my devouring of the literature was any serious sense of agency on the part of what was still called the Third World, neither in political nor organizational nor philosophical terms. I also missed any serious treatment of religion—something that is a clear embarrassment from today's fraught standpoint. I penned a clearly polemical and questioning article. R. J. Vincent, then editor of the *Review of International Studies*, had befriended me and said he was inclined to publish it—as a provocation if nothing else. He then tragically and suddenly died. His successors did not publish it and it eventually appeared in the journal founded by University of Kent students, *Paradigms*, the ancestor of what is now *Global Society*.[14]

I had a little bit of consciousness-raising from my head of department, Professor John (A. J. R.) Groom: "If you're going to keep doing this (writing such articles) you'd better keep publishing work on Africa too as a professional shield. This could get controversial." So I proceeded on a twin track. As John advised I set about becoming an authority particularly on Southern Africa,[15] and on the political meaning of Zambia's President Kenneth Kaunda—who hosted several liberation groups in his country[16]— and Zimbabwe's President Robert Mugabe.[17] But I also published a long stream of articles on alternative world lenses for viewing IR and even, at one International Studies Association convention in Chicago, introduced my paper with silent Tibetan *mudra* or hand gestures. This activity culminated in two books, the first popular enough to be listed in one category as a *Guardian* newspaper book of the year,[18] and the second with sufficient policy weight to attract a bulk order from the U.S. Department of State.[19] But the greatest pleasure in all of this was to see the "cause" taken up by better scholars, such as Lily Ling and Anna Agathangelou.[20] Others, more eminent, are now writing about different starting points for conceiving the international.[21] Lately I have been specialising in the resacralised nature of IR. This resacralisation has come about whether IR liked it or not, and whether it was prepared for it or not (it wasn't),[22] and that is because of the advent of *jihad* as a new internationalism.[23]

RECEIVING AND CONTESTING THE NATIONAL

Also in more recent years I became, unwillingly, involved in the debate on China and Africa. In a way this merged the twin tracks I had instigated following John Groom's advice. How to understand the Chinese, and how to understand Africa. My presupposition in both cases is that there is deep thought. My book on the subject also became listed in the *Guardian* newspaper's books of the year.[24] It was written to be part of public debate. By that time, by virtue of being both Chinese and an Africanist, I had been included in a high-level African negotiating delegation visiting Beijing, led by the deputy chair of the African Union.

Unwillingly, because I had never felt comfortable being Chinese. And this was because my condition of being Chinese was tempered by being the first-born son of refugees to New Zealand. Tempered like a sword is tempered. Discrimination made it hard.[25] There were cartoons of innocent Maori maidens being corrupted by the rapacious pig-tailed Chinese octopus.[26] But it was far from impossible, as New Zealand remained a land of opportunities. But you did have to be better than everyone else. I did achieve this academically and in such intellectual sphere as the country had, but still came second in every major international scholarship competition the country hosted. It was decades after me before there was a first Chinese Rhodes Scholar from New Zealand. But I did not want the tempered blade to cut as a Chinese. I felt alienated from the diasporic community. I had received no support from it in my political and intellectual activities. I was instead frowned upon for not keeping my head down and behaving in a sedate way that would invite less discrimination against the community as a whole. Stuart Grief used me as the key but lone example in his Berkeley PhD thesis of politicised rebellion among the New Zealand Chinese.[27] I found such Chinese identity as I could manage in the dawning of the kung fu movie era—martial arts was the only thing that bound me to my grandmother, who had been a kung fu militia leader in the warlord era[28]—and became myself a well-known karate exponent. The poem I wrote about the strange pride that resulted is still taught in New Zealand universities.[29]

"Watch How the Chinese Walk"

watch how the Chinese walk
out of kung fu movies
their elbows are bent
one foot works like an anchor
the skinniest Chinese
looks awesome

when the Chinese walk
out of kung fu movies
they feel awesome
the oldest are glad
to know at last
the joy of assuming say
the gait of the frontier marshal
the stride of steve reeves

when the Chinese walk
out of kung fu movies
they feel able to fly
at least across the street
to leap
at least as high as first
floor awnings

watch how the Chinese walk
out of kung fu movies
every six-foot 200-pound pakeha
keeps respectful distance

A *pakeha* is a white man in the Maori language. And, if I felt ambivalent about being diasporic Chinese, I felt drawn to the Maori cause. The indigenous people of *Aotearoa*—the Land of the Long White Cloud—before it was renamed New Zealand, had clearly become an underclass, suffering simultaneous discrimination and patronage. They had a history as "noble savages," resisting white colonialism and land grabs with valour and chivalry. This was admired. Gallant losers. But after they had been defeated, they went into decline. As a child I saw they were treated as unhygienic and financially disorganised, as having no modern future. It was my first lesson in realising there were people poorer than my Chinese family, as I watched my father—working in his parents' fruit shop—setting aside each day a tray of free fruit for the local Maori children. They came in very politely, with big grins, without shoes and wearing tattered clothes. I remember being four and being scandalised. So, as a student I became the media adviser to the newly formed *nga tamatoa*, the Young Warriors, modeled on the Black Panthers in the United States. It was the start of a huge renaissance, first in pride, then in political assertion. When I became a newspaper editor, I published the country's first newspaper headline in Maori language. And, later, wrote a book of poems entitled *Songs of the Maori King*.[30] It was about the existential despair of Potatau I, elected King of the Maoris to lead the resistance. Already there had been huge missionary influence so, in Biblical fashion, Potatau went into the forest for forty days and nights to meditate and draw up his strength. In the final poem in the cycle, I have him realising he must fight, but he faced a stronger enemy. It is a poem about accepting fate, and fighting anyway.

"Potatau's Song of Battle"

The trees and the birds are melting and weeping
into a sparse and dribbling civility.

There is an end to the tether. Who could tell?
But that there should have been innumerable rescues,

bold and daring, charged with the warmth of forgetfulness,
sweeping aside this subjugation.
The hours close. The dreams of chivalry vanish.
What markings adorn our faces now . . . what gauntlets

guard our wrists and flaming rings band round
our heads?

The Maori King, his single self, now stands before the storm.
He stares about, broken, at distances, empty-eyed

but seeking magic mirrors in each sun's stroke of native land.
From the trees of the white man

red leaves of autumn burn or bleed into the earth.
Their grand final colour is their grand final gesture.

I shall collect gestures, these cold days that come.
I must try as winter sweeps slowly in. I must not

fail the young men at arms, as they carve a great season.
Though this morning I awoke, to imagine they had all

become the impenetrable sky, a wide membrane
burning scarlet into an eternity of unrecompensed sorrow.

There is an end to the tether. I perceive the tightening
and gathering in of all our lives.

We, without exception, are wound in cords of red and vermillion.
Wrapped and bundled for some universal arbiter.

He will see our lines and know our history.

It's come to this pathos, whichever deities oversee me—I mock you.
I am sorry. As much I mock myself.

I look around me. It is a great widened world. We confront
it on our borders. We are stretched to emptiness.

I craft no visions of deliverance. I must return to the
young men and old warriors, drilling before the armoured gates.

Ancestral spirits sweep round in clusters.
Broken men catch broken spirits as they urge on the rescue.
Do not see them from far-off hills.

Fighting anyway, despite overwhelming odds. As the U.S. B52s dropped their tonnage on North Vietnam and 500,000 U.S. troops fought in South Vietnam, atrocities were committed on both sides—but the killing of villagers by American soldiers at My Lai horrified the world. The New Zealand poem that captured the default casualness that allowed each soldier to do this was by David Mitchell, in his ground-breaking book which I was able to publish with book design innovations not previously seen in the country (basically financed from bank overdrafts which I could not really repay—the banks knew this—as I was still a student). Here is an excerpt:[31]

> & he
> sits in th kitchen
> playing poker with his mates
> & he
> contemplates his hand
> & he
> holds a king
> to each soft lip
> in turn
>
> & th others pass
> (& he waits his turn)
>
> & 30 seconds pass
> & he
> plays his hand
> &
> children burn.

Of course the casual racism that back-dropped slaughter was appalling. I became an anti-war activist and helped lead the storming of the U.S. Consulate for New Zealand's first sit-in. We were arrested but, with the help of the University of Auckland School of Law, I mounted a civil liberties defence in court—to no avail, although the magistrate did impose lenient sentences. But I published many poems. Some called upon the older Chinese community at least to recognise what was going on in an Asian country. Here is an excerpt from one such long poem.[32]

> Dear Mother & Father,
> What if those had been my uncles and aunts,

all of us with the yellow skins
of a blood-warmed earth?
What if those yellow bodies
floating down the wide rivers of
Viet Nam, Laos, Cambodia,
had been ours?

The poems of this sort were without nuance or poetic distance. They were meant to be public interventions. They did not persuade the Chinese public at least. On demonstration after demonstration I would be the only Asian face. I grew my hair over my shoulders, took to wearing frock coats and silk bandanas to make myself more conspicuous. If there was going to be only one, let the cameras capture him and allow the impression there might be others. Probably the most direct and deliberately affecting of such poems was published in a political as opposed to literary journal.[33]

"Vietnam Girl"

Forgive me little Vietnamese girl
for all the time I pretended
there was no evidence
of your rape.

Forgive me for ever thinking
there could be threads
for a new universe
while you writhed
in a napalm dance.

All that is left is the fire
and the hate
and the love we bombed into
oblivion.

Forgive me little Vietnamese girl
for living in a nation
that helped to
destroy your smiles
leaving only a blank eternity.

In the name of humanity
we took away your humanity
took away your loveliness
and reduced you to a faceless statistic
for historians to wonder at.

In my nation
there are also little girls
that no one could ever think of raping.
While you are raped
by the weapons of war
and our guilt defiles your innocence.

In my nation
there are men who lament
the destruction of sonnets and ballads.
But who could ever rewrite
your unfilled beauty of life?

And the callousness of it all
is the callousness of my nation
who makes much
of a treaty paper
but cares nothing for you.

Forgive me little Vietnamese girl
for all the time I pretended
there was no evidence
of your rape.

Forgive me if you can
for being unable
to stop my government
from raping your sister
tomorrow.

But, in the new competitiveness of the literary world, which was also under-going a renaissance just as we were seeking to forge a political renaissance, I did try to publish something more technically poetic—but still with a clear message.[34]

"A Spirit Medical for Fall or Strick"

Leung Choy Sun
my noble ancestor
in a commissioned hour
devised a wondrous spirit
      Tin-Chat
      Frankincense
      Heung Foo
      Ge-Je

Tinctzingeber
Jack-Lan
Kwai-San
Chat-Chur
Hung Far
Peach Nut
       and presented his formula
       too overcome with red poppies
       reaping a royal citation
       for his efforts
and i young enough
to be sealed over
with grief
       working like a sweated alchemist
       pouring through his scripture
       have rediscovered the combination
       correct in all its quantities
and allowing myself absolution every night
with its fragrance
do not merely chance to see
my ancestor's body
floating down a Cambodian river.

The bulk of my poetry at the time were the love songs of a young man—although the best known of the books did contrive to use what we called "oriental" imagery.[35] But the sending of New Zealand artillery battalions to Vietnam made for a fraying last straw. As did my public argument with Robert Muldoon, the prime minister—absurd that he should pay attention to a lone Asian person. I had achieved a reputation. I had discovered a vocation—one had to fight for peace and equality—but the country was becoming too small. To be considered a leading public intellectual figure by age twenty-five was ridiculous. I made plans to move on. The final choice was between London University and the Sorbonne. I threw a dart. It landed on London. But, as John Groom later intuited, my upbringing would always haunt me and keep me at an edge of complete acceptability wherever I went.[36]

NOTES

1. Brian Porter, "David Davies: A Hunter after Peace," *Review of International Studies*, 15:1, 1989, pp 27–36.

2. Michael Banks, "The Inter-Paradigm Debate," in Margot Light & A. J. R. Groom (eds.), *International Relations: A Handbook of Current Theory*, London: Frances Pinter, 1985, pp 7–26.

3. Thomas S. Kuhn, *The Structure of Scientific Revolutions*, Chicago: University of Chicago Press, 1970.

4. For example, Michael Smith, Richard Little, & Michael Shackleton (eds.), *Perspectives on World Politics*, London: Croom Helm, 1981.

5. For example, albeit with a slight genuflection to developmental dependency thought at the end, Karl W. Deutsch, *The Analysis of International Relations*, Englewood Cliffs, NJ: Prentice-Hall, 1978.

6. Klaus Knorr & James N. Rosenau (eds.), *Contending Approaches to International Politics*, Princeton, NJ: Princeton University Press, 1969.

7. Hedley Bull, *The Anarchical Society: A Study of Order in World Politics*, London: Palgrave Macmillan, 2002 (first published 1977). Hans J. Morgenthau, *Politics among Nations: The Struggle for Power and Peace*, New York: Knopf, 1968.

8. Chris Brown, *International Relations Theory: New Normative Approaches*, Hemel Hempstead: Harvester Wheatsheaf, 1992.

9. Christine Sylvester, *Feminist Theory and International Relations in a Postmodern Era*, Cambridge, UK: Cambridge University Press, 1994.

10. This was first published as the prelude to my novel, *Joseph Kony and the Titans of Zagreb*, London: Nth Position, 2012, pp 1–4.

11. Stephen Chan, *Issues in International Relations: A View from Africa*, London: Macmillan, 1987.

12. Willy Brandt, *North-South: A Programme for Survival*, London: Pan, 1980.

13. Fred Halliday, *Cold War Third World*, London: Radius, 1991.

14. Stephen Chan, "A Summer Polemic: Revolution, Rebellion, and Romance: Some Notes Towards the Resacralisation of I.R.," *Paradigms: The Kent Journal of International Relations*, 7:1, 1993, pp 85–100.

15. Stephen Chan, *Southern Africa: Old Treacheries and New Deceits*, New Haven, CT: Yale University Press, 2011.

16. Stephen Chan, *Kaunda and Southern Africa: Image and Reality in Foreign Policy*, London: I. B. Tauris, 1992.

17. Stephen Chan, *Robert Mugabe: A Life of Power and Violence*, Ann Arbor: University of Michigan Press, 2002. Stephen Chan & Julia Gallagher, *Why Mugabe Won: The 2013 Elections in Zimbabwe and Their Aftermath*, Cambridge, UK: Cambridge University Press, 2017.

18. Stephen Chan, *The End of Certainty: Towards a New Internationalism*, London: Zed, 2009.

19. Stephen Chan, *Plural International Relations in a Divided World*, Cambridge, UK: Polity, 2017.

20. See Anna M. Agathangelou & L. H. M. Ling, *Transforming World Politics: From Empire to Multiple Worlds*, Abingdon: Routledge, 2009. The late Lily Ling published a stream of important and illustrative works, beginning with L. H. M. Ling, *Postcolonial International Relations: Conquest and Desire between Asia and the West*, Houndmills: Palgrave Macmillan, 2002.

21. Barry Buzan, & Amitav Acharya, *The Making of Global International Relations*, Cambridge, UK: Cambridge University Press, 2019.

22. An important exception is Fabio Petito. See *inter alia* Luca Avelli & Fabio Petito (eds.), *Towards a Postsecular International Politics: New Forms of Community, Identity, and Power*, New York: Palgrave Macmillan, 2014.

23. Stephen Chan, *Spear to the West: Thought and Recruitment in Violent Jihadism*, London: Hurst, 2019.

24. Stephen Chan (ed.), *The Morality of China in Africa: The Middle Kingdom and the Dark Continent*, London: Zed, 2013.

25. For the accounts of early Chinese families, including my own, see: Manying Ip, *Dragons of the Long White Cloud: The Making of Chinese New Zealanders*, Auckland: Tandem, 1996. A photograph of my cousins adorns the front cover.

26. Manying Ip & Nigel Murphy, *Aliens at My Table: Asians as New Zealanders see Them*, Auckland: Penguin, 2005.

27. Stuart W. Grief, *The Overseas Chinese in New Zealand*, Singapore: Asia Pacific Press, 1974, pp 126–131.

28. https://chinesemartialstudies.com/2015/08/02/prof-stephen-chan-discusses-the-life-of-chan-wong-wah-yue-warlord-era-swordswoman-village-militia-member-and-grandmother/, 20 June 2020.

29. Stephen Chan, "Watch How the Chinese Walk," *Landfall*, 115, 1975, p 226. Anthologised in Vaughan Rapatahana (ed.), *Poetry in Multicultural Oceania*, Invercargill: Essential Resources, 2019.

30. Stephen Chan, *Songs of the Maori King*, Victoria: Sono Nis Press (then the poetry arm of the University of British Columbia Press), 1986.

31. David Mitchell, "ponsonby/remuera/my lai," in David Mitchell, *Pipe Dreams in Ponsonby*, Auckland: Association of Orientally Flavoured Syndics, 1972, first poem of the second section, no page number.

32. For example, Stephen Chan, "A Renunciation of Guiltlessness," *Edge*, 4, 1972, pp 31–33. Anthologised in Alan Brunton, Murray Edmond, & Michele Leggott (eds.), *Big Smoke: New Zealand Poems, 1960–1975*, Auckland: Auckland University Press, 2000, pp 219–222.

33. Stephen Chan, "Vietnam Girl," *New Zealand Monthly Review*, X:109, 1970, p 5. Anthologised in Elsie Locke, *Peace People: A History of Peace Activities in New Zealand*, Christchurch: Hazard, 1992, pp 242–243.

34. Stephen Chan, "A Spirit Medical for Fall or Strick," *Mate*, 20, 1972, p 25. Anthologised in Brunton, Edmond, Leggott, *op.cit.*, pp 218–219.

35. Stephen Chan, *Arden's Summer*, Christchurch: Pegasus, 1975, ends with a genuflection to ancient poet Li Po.

36. A fictional recreation of these early influences and how they developed may be found in the four novellas of Stephen Chan, *The White Door*, London: Nth Position, 2012.

Chapter 2

Facing the International

I reached London in the latter part of the 1976 heat wave—at least it was a heat wave in British terms—but Britain was even then unprepared for things out of the ordinary. All public administration was predicated on regularity and "normality." Water became scarce. The fabled lawns dried up. At that point, many people did not bathe every day—in the heat wave they couldn't anyway—but that made my learning to use the London underground aromatic. I arrived at King's College, the second oldest part of the University of London, founded as a rival to Jeremy Bentham's University College. It was full of *hauteur* and an impersonation or professorial memory of Oxbridge standards. The work load was horrendous. It was for the fabled King's MA in war studies, an almost archaic international relations with what we would now call strategic studies. I learned from briefly shared intelligence reports that the Soviets had targeted central London with five nuclear warheads—one of course aimed at Whitehall and Parliament; one at the BBC in Bush House next door to King's. Being at the planned epi-centre of vaporization, after the blue seas and skies of New Zealand, made for an interesting transition. The MA had recruited a select group of just over twenty students, almost all from overseas; they included senior military officers; there were probably two left wing students, one an Australian and one myself. My colleague students were by and large cordial—not all my professors were. So I sought to learn by immersion British manners and restraint, as well as quaint habits to do with passing the port when a guest in an officer's mess. We were all granted associate membership of the military think tank, the Royal United Services Institute in Whitehall, another Soviet bomb target, and I learned the thinking of military men—at that stage, no women could be seen wearing stars on their epaulets. I would drift from King's to RUSI, Trafalgar square being the marker between two straight routes, and itself another bomb target. The security desk at RUSI got used to my long hair and Cuban heels—but I was always revengefully mindful, as recompense for careful behaviour, that outside had been the scaffold where Charles I had been executed. If it was

17

a cultural education, the academic experience was rich and, for me, torrid. Almost no one agreed with my positions on world politics. Or even my view that the Chinese classics could enrich our knowledge of strategy. These days everyone reads Sun Tzu, but they didn't then.[1]

Finally, the end was within sight. It was time to write the end-of-year dissertation. I was the only one to choose an African topic. I knew that the Commonwealth Secretariat in Pall Mall, in Marlborough House at the end of the long line of gentlemen's clubs, had files I needed to consult. I had a distant friend who was a senior figure in the Secretariat's Legal Division. He asked me to visit him and he would arrange access for me. We were sitting in his office, making small talk, when his telephone rang. It was the director of another division. He had just discovered a terrible mess in the filing systems of his own office. He calculated it would take six weeks to sort. "Do you know anyone who could come in on an emergency assignment for six weeks?" My friend began laughing and said, "The person you need is sitting opposite me. He was president of the national students' association in New Zealand, then a newspaper editor. I'd say that after one week he could come in and do this for you." Then he turned to me and said, "Finish your dissertation, go and buy a new suit, be behind the desk in the office they will provide for you at this time next week." I'm not sure I had very much say in any of this.

The Commonwealth Secretariat, especially under Secretary-General Shridath Ramphal, the eminent Guyanese diplomatic figure (and King's graduate), had become something transformed from memories of the British Commonwealth that was meant to hold sway after the British Empire. In 1947, newly independent India had refused to join anything labeled "British." At Indian insistence it became the Commonwealth of Nations with all members being equal and without British leadership. The Secretariat was established as its independent coordinating arm, but Ramphal made it a leadership institution. He prioritised freedom in Southern Africa as a main Commonwealth goal, and international economic reform as a major cause.[2] Then, it was briefly a Rolls Royce organization, even as the Foreign and Commonwealth Office started ceasing to be so. To be asked to join it, even briefly, was considered an honour. For me, it was an accident. After six weeks, they asked me to stay. I bought yet another new suit and told King's I would have to do my PhD part-time. But my unorthodox landing in the Secretariat caused resentment among the existing staffers. They made life very hard for me and I was plunged unwillingly into the institutional power plays that made their New Zealand equivalents seem primitive. The New Zealand High Commission kindly rode some shotgun for me. I was happy another New Zealander had been employed in the Secretariat but, as I took up my position, the High Commission called me in and said the New Zealand government had given the Secretariat security clearance for my employment. "You see," the young diplomat quietly explained, "It took longer than usual—you do have, er, an unusual record—but it came from the Prime Minister himself. It reads, 'if you want Stephen Chan, you can HAVE him.' You make powerful enemies, Stephen. You must find a way to maintain your convictions and make more subtle your behaviour." Thus began a life-long lesson which I have not completely mastered.

The High Commission also issued me a passport with special numbers—as I was to be employed at a lower level than that which would qualify for a diplomatic passport. "This might help you out of problems in foreign parts." In fact, it caused me very many problems. The numbers, I discovered much later, were a code that was meant to afford some kind of *laissez passer*—for international intelligence operatives. All they did was to ensure I became a veteran of airport interrogations, clearly as a spy. "Why does this keep happening?" I would ask myself.

A small number of senior figures in the Secretariat befriended me. One was Moni Malhoutra, director of Ramphal's private office. He had come first out of 2 million entrants in the Indian civil service exams. He was brilliant and decisive—and very knowing that he was so. As the war against white rule intensified in Rhodesia, the Secretariat, especially Ramphal's office, played an increasing role in forming a diplomatic front for the free states of Southern Africa, all supportive of liberation. All antagonised by the British policy of opposition to white rule while achieving nothing substantial in reining it in. It would be Moni who would involve me in all of this. But, first, there were two preparatory lessons in other theatres.

POLITE BLOOD AND THE POLITICS OF BLOOD

I didn't realise in 1979 how important my visits to Sri Lanka and Thailand were. The Secretariat mounted a conference of young Commonwealth Leaders, organised by its own Youth Programme. Even if only two of us on the staff of this Programme were actually young—still in our twenties—it was better than the spectacle that greeted me in Colombo, where the Minister of Youth from Bangladesh was in his eighties.

There were, however, two key features about this conference. It was held just before the UNCTAD V negotiations in Manila—crucial talks to resolve disagreements about international trade and finance. Several delegations bound for Manila decided to use Colombo as a stopover, both to overcome jet lag before flying on to very difficult negotiations and also to discuss their positions with other delegations. The second feature was that the Sri Lankan government hosts were extremely young ministers—a much touted golden generation, some also still in their twenties or early thirties. But looming over their country was the spectre of war as the Tamil Tigers began their mobilization. Not that you could notice in the splendours of the seaside Oberoi Hotel with its vast atrium. What did belie the apparently advanced luxury was the fact that Sri Lanka was still essentially a cash economy. I was the assistant secretary of the meeting, and part of my job was to uplift the funds sent from the Secretariat in London to pay for all the local staff and facilities. As in a gangster movie, the leather valise containing millions in local notes was handcuffed to my wrist and I walked like that from the bank to the hotel, hoping not to attract too much attention. But I did get to know the young ministers. I suggested to the minister of youth that he host a birthday party for his Zambian counterpart, Kebby Musokotwane, turning thirty-three in Colombo, and he did so. Kebby later became Zambian minister of finance and prime minister, and negotiated with the IMF so successfully that political jealousies overthrew him even as he was flying back home from Washington, DC. But, as the years went by, one by one the young Sri Lankan ministers were exploded by Tamil Tiger bombs. The minister of youth, Ranil Wickramasinghe, survived. In 1979, his was the most junior position, he was the most handsome of the ministers, and was accounted a playboy. He became the only prime minister to seriously seek to end the war and, for a short time, was successful, before, again, political struggles for his government and war resumed. He returned to office many years later, after war ended in a savage victory for the government in Colombo and some process of healing had to begin. But, in 1979, he arranged for me to be part of a small group to interview the then Prime Minister Ranasinghe Premadasa. It is now clear that Premadasa was part of a Buddhist nationalist project to subjugate the Tamil Hindu minority.[3] In 1979, he projected an air of Buddhist serenity. I rose to speak and said that the international community was deeply concerned by the possibility of extreme violence, and that surely it was still not too late for his government to seek negotiations rather than mobilise its force. I was then subjected to a masterclass in Buddhist condescension and serene chiding. I never forgot it. "Young man," he began, and then I was advised, serenely, not to interfere in things too complex for me, and indeed the world, to understand.

On the eve of the conference's end, I was desperately tired. It was very late and I was almost alone in the atrium, drinking vodka and coconut milk out of a hollowed coconut. The minister from Lesotho and his assistant approached me. "We are flying to Manila tomorrow for the UNCTAD." I wished them a safe flight and thanked them for coming. "We have to present our country's position paper on international trade. All the delegations must present such a paper." This would have been normal. "We have no paper. No one in Lesotho was equipped to write such a paper." I looked up and knew what they wanted—and went away and wrote their paper. But I was learning the perfidies of the world and the inadequacies of very many who suffered them.

Fighting back, pushing back, depends on knowledge, and the application of knowledge depends on strategy. Alliances make strategy work. Alliances have no place for passengers. If you don't have knowledge to contribute you are a passenger—and the vexatious circle is completed.

If Sri Lanka was a lesson in the basic political mechanics, and their lack of necessity for constant moral foundations, what happened next was a lesson in Buddhist serenity, minus the nationalism. The New Zealand government asked me to fly from Sri Lanka to Thailand. The attempt by the Thai army to crush a student rebellion had only resulted in thousands of students taking to the hills and taking up arms. New Zealand aid projects were close to the zones of conflict. The deputy ambassador was prepared to drive up-country to ascertain their safety. Would I accompany him?

I would, but getting into Thailand was an exercise with ironies. It was not my passport numbers but my profiling as a possible drug smuggler. I was carrying a carving, a wooden Sri Lankan demon—a gift from Wickramasinghe. Thailand was then a key exporter of illicit drugs so it felt very rich to be accused at customs of smuggling into Thailand a carving that was "patently" made from solid marijuana. Thankfully, the deputy ambassador appeared airside with his immunity passes and carted me, with my demon, to the embassy compound. I had a day to become accustomed to the climate, even more humid than Sri Lanka, and my accommodation being in Patpong, the red-light district, I would be pursued down the streets, taken as a rich Singapore businessman, with all manner of sexual offerings. The more I quickened my pace, the more exotic the offers became. I was, I thought, very worldly, but was taken aback. "Do people do that?" was my resonant thought as I sifted the menus, apparatus, five genders of all age groups, and combinations available, with or without service animals. Complete with discounts for multiple use.

Escaping Bangkok for the jungles north of the city was a relief. But mid-trip was my thirtieth birthday. We were first stranded by a violent monsoon. When it abated, we found an open air restaurant in a jungle clearing near Udorn. The waiters brought many large bottles of beer and a vast number of dishes. As soon as they put the food down, our table was attacked by huge squadrons of gigantic flies from the jungle. We couldn't beat them off. I saw the waiters were laughing. Finally, they came and explained. We were to sit on one side of the table. On the other side, they lined up a long row of beer bottle caps. In every alternate cap they put a morsel of food, and filled the other with beer. Then they stood back. The flies came and ate and drank only from their placings. We kept refilling the bottle caps and they never disturbed us for the duration of my party. As we were leaving, one waiter explained: "Buddhist flies." It was to set the tone for our observation of what had been designated a war zone.

That tone was that violence could be both surreal and highly mannered. Placement in the zone of conflict was everything. It was like a chessboard. When two students mounted on a Kawasaki burst out of the jungle, the pillion passenger carrying an AK47, both masked, we knew we were in student territory. A kilometre further on, we would confront an army patrol, the soldiers in dark glasses, chrome helmets, and standing to attention on the tray of a slow-moving truck, carrying new American assault rifles with fixed bayonets, helmets, and bayonets gleaming in the sun. We were demonstrably in army territory. Each side had squares of the jungle. Neither side transgressed into the other's squares. We were sometimes inspected by one or the other side, but no one showed any interest in hindering us. Their interest was in maintaining a war of symbolic occupations of space. They had no interest in open conflict. In due course, a blanket amnesty was promulgated, and the students returned to their universities, both sides able to claim they had not given an inch. All honour was preserved. Buddhist rebellion. I reasoned that in an actual conflict I would do well to introduce some elements of theatre and relief from reality. The chance to do that came sooner than I thought, as the war of liberation in Rhodesia took dramatic turns—not so much on the battlefield where a fierce war of attrition was slowly turning the tide, though far from decisively, in favour of the guerrillas, but in the corridors of power and diplomacy.

ENDGAME AND PEACE IN ZIMBABWE

My interest in the liberation of what became Zimbabwe began in 1969, when, after being arrested for occupying the U.S. Consulate in Auckland, my police cell was opposite that of Henderson Tapela—who had joined the protest and also been arrested. The New Zealand government had provided no scholarships for refugee students, so the national student association did. Henderson was one of two students from Rhodesia studying in New Zealand under such scholarships. Through the small grills in our cell doors, we struck up an immediate friendship. "You know," he said, "we must protest iniquity, that's why I joined you today, but let me tell you about the struggle in my own country." Years later, when I was supervising the observation of the independence election campaign in a black suburb of Bulawayo, a woman came rushing up to me. "You're Stephen Chan! You don't know me. I know you because you are exactly the description my brother gave me. I am Henderson's sister!" By then, independence under majority rule was close. But there was still huge tension in the air, so the sisterly intervention immediately established my *bona fides* in the crowd. Of the election observation, more later. Before then, back in New Zealand, I was elected president of the NZ University Students' Association. This was more than it seemed. I had more than twenty staff on salaries, honoraria, or retainers. I chaired the board of an international airline that chartered its jets to transport overseas students to and from Australia and Malaysia. We dealt in seven-figure sums. But we also hosted a lecture tour in 1973 by the legendary liberation leader, Herbert Chitepo. My vice president, Alex Shaw, did the honours on that one. If Chitepo had lived—but he was assassinated before independence came to Zimbabwe, it would not have been Mugabe who led the country.[4] So, by the time I joined the Secretariat, I was deeply aware of its agenda, and already what might have been, to help achieve the end of white minority rule in the country then named after Cecil Rhodes.

The spark for serious diplomatic movement was in fact provided by Margaret Thatcher, who, fresh in office, contemplated recognizing a compromise white/black government in Rhodesia—even though the black side was patently cosmetic. Even this had been forced on the white minority government because of guerrilla advances. Lord Carrington, Thatcher's foreign secretary, was aghast.[5] Although the two men basically hated each other, Carrington and Ramphal worked together toward the 1979 Commonwealth summit in Lusaka where, helped by the adroit chairmanship of host President Kaunda, and a long line of basically handsome and charming Commonwealth leaders paying court on Thatcher, it was agreed to force negotiations of all parties at Lancaster House in London. The one dissenting Commonwealth leader, New Zealand's Robert Muldoon, was frozen out and—to my utmost satisfaction—spent most of the summit brooding in his villa.

Lancaster House is grand and its magnificent staircase leading to the spacious ballrooms used for the negotiations was foreboding. Walking up them for leaders of a guerrilla war or of a rebel government with the capacity for provincial administration was almost a deliberate lesson in humility. To keep up a string of such psychological pressures, Lord Carrington chaired the negotiations ruthlessly.[6] Shadowing the talks, Ramphal convened the Commonwealth High Commissioners accredited to London in almost daily sessions. It was called the Commonwealth Committee on Southern Africa, and its chief intent was to prevent Carrington from forcing too great a compromise upon the guerrilla leaders. Moni Malhoutra saw me lurking outside the doors of the conference room one day. Marlborough House, where the high commissioners convened, was almost as grand as Lancaster House a stone's throw away. I had no business being outside the conference room. Moni grinned, and gestured me in, pointed to a chair a row behind the conference table; afterward he just said, "come every day if you want." It was the first time anyone senior in the Secretariat had declared some trust in me.

The amusing side of it occurred when one day I was assigned to greet Joshua Nkomo, the leader of one of the two liberation movements, coming to discuss negotiating tactics with Ramphal. I met him and his two aides in the entrance hall of Marlborough House. Nkomo was a capacious man. Marlborough House was under conservation orders. Modern elevators could not be installed. There was a single very old and very narrow lift to Ramphal's office. I could just fit in with Nkomo. I smiled at his two aides: "You need to greet your man as he comes out of the lift. It's two floors up. The lift is slow. It will be slower now. You'd better, all the same, start running." Breathlessly they were awaiting their man as the ramshackle iron cage finally laboured its way to Ramphal's floor. It was said that the ghost of Queen Mary went up and down in that lift every night when all human life had departed. I didn't tell the superstitious Nkomo that. He would have been more breathless than his aides if he had elected to climb the stairs.

The Lancaster House negotiations were difficult, tense, and often on a knife's edge.[7] Finally it was agreed that the guerrilla parties would be legalised, the opposed armies would observe a ceasefire monitored by Commonwealth army contingents, an election would be held with open campaigning by all candidates, including those recently outlawed and under threat of being shot on sight. Ramphal ensured a late insertion in the agreement that the elections would be observed independently of any arrangements made by a newly installed, temporary but very powerful British governor.[8] After elections and a majority rule government, independence would come at the beginning of March 1980. Campaigning and the move in from the bush would start at the beginning of January 1980. It was now December 1979.[9]

Even though not directly involved in the negotiations I was exhausted. I had shadowed them not only at Marlborough House, but with the guerrilla contingents who had accompanied their leaders to London. Sometimes, when it seemed the talks would fail, when it seemed Carrington would push too hard in the direction of the white government, the mood would be ominous. The talk was of a return to war. I decided to spend Christmas and New Year's Day in Algeria with a busload of Spanish Civil War veterans, International Brigade members from Britain, who were drawn to the fact that the bus would pass through Madrid where they had made their last stand before defeat. It was to be itself an emotional visit. They found the remains of the trenches where they had stood and fought. In Algeria, in the oasis of Ain Sefra just beyond the Atlas Mountains, as if weighed down by a premonition, I thought I should stay there. I had the sense my life would change if I returned to London. There is a photograph of my footsteps disappearing across and beyond a great dune in the Sahara.

Sure enough, when I returned there was a handwritten note in pencil on my desk. It was from Moni. It said I should not unpack. I was to be helping lead the reconnaissance of Rhodesia for what became the Commonwealth Observer Group. No one had observed an election of this sort before. No one had any idea how to do it. No one had any real idea of the lie of the land in Rhodesia, nor how dangerous it would be if the ceasefire did not hold. The reconnaissance group had a week in the country to make something up and submit it to Moni who would descend with the senior observers. Getting to Rhodesia took a dog-leg of flights. In the layover at Amsterdam and its shopping mall of an airport, it suddenly struck me that—as my only preparation for the sudden trip had been a hasty visit to Regent Street to buy sturdy clothes (suitable only for shooting quail in Scotland), including a jacket with shotgun cartridge loops on the inside—I should buy several dozen Cuban cigars.

Rhodesia from the start was a frenetic whirlwind. Peter Snelson and I were given the task of reconnoitring the entire country. We divided it between us. In what was going to be the western headquarters of observation, Bulawayo, I booked every rental car and light aircraft available. It was like a throwback to New Zealand at the local airport. "Will that be self-fly, sir?" I swallowed hard and asked for pilots. Basically, the plan that emerged was to establish regional hubs, with coordinators or secretariat on site, and the senior observers would, in small groups, rotate from week to week from hub to hub. The coordinators were to set up and facilitate extensive itineraries for each week's group. In a country recently at war and without full infrastructure, or proper roads once off the highways, with landmines and armed dissidents on all sides, this was more easily said than done. It was nonetheless done. There were some very senior figures among the observers, many of whom had not tasted rough conditions for decades, if at all. Their chairman, a distinguished Indian ambassador, Rajeshwar Dayal, forestalled complaint by immediately leading the way.[10] With Emmanuel Apea, I was told to coordinate the west from Bulawayo. The area covered was the size of England. I pinned a huge map of the provinces, Matabeleland North and Matabeleland South to our improvised operations room wall and stuck pins into 100 locations. "We have to say we got to every one of these."

I have written about what all this entailed, and how it was done, elsewhere.[11] All that should be repeated here are a handful of the stories, and some of the poems that arose from them. Some stories I have told so often they are hackneyed—such as eating with a brace of Mugabe's Chinese-trained officers, all of us using chopsticks. A less-told story was learning how to fly a Cessna aircraft. We worked our pilot so hard he would sometimes slump asleep at the controls, muttering the words, "you fly this thing, you've watched me enough, wake me up when we need to land . . ." Learning to fly is an exaggeration of course. Monitoring the altimeter and compass, and steering a course at an appropriate height was all I had to do. But it was a light relief from other activities—except when the aircraft was driven down by torrential rain and storms and we tried to crash land in a flooded field. The pilot was firmly back at the controls for that but was screaming for instructions as we touched down and turned into a power boat. I told him to abort the attempted landing and pull back the throttle. We were going to ride out the storm. The two black Commonwealth colonels in the backseat were now passing for white.

But the real drama, and the psychological exercise of reducing it to a normality, was on the ground. I recall, many years later, watching the film, *The Last King of Scotland*, and involuntarily pulling back in my seat. It was an early scene where the young doctor looks up to see a semi-circle of soldiers with their assault rifles pointed at him. It was an interesting trigger, to use a weak pun. In my case, the AK47s would be pointed at my chest. These weapons have a savage kickback so, if they fired, I would lose my head. At the best of times their consequences are rather messy. At such moments the scan for minute details becomes the alarming part. Whether their safety catches are off. Whether they have in fact filed away their safety catches. Whether they were as old as seventeen, younger. Which one was the commanding officer? That last question was key, and that was where the cigars came into their own. I would very slowly and ostentatiously open my jacket. Remove a cigar from its cartridge loop and offer it to the unit commander. Mutter the words, "Che Guevara . . ." Then slowly take out my lighter. Gesture to him to cup his hands around the cigar while I lit it. This would be a huge success, as he took both hands off his gun. I then passed cigars around and slowly explained that we were observers and, since we were in Nkomo's heartland, explain how I had met the man himself—without describing the farce of the tiny lift.

They were meant to have disarmed when leaving their designated ceasefire assembly points. But the Rhodesian security forces didn't either when they left their own barracks. But white brigadiers and black commanders were immaculately polite. I made white soldiers salute the Nigerian colonel who frequently accompanied me. And I would take solace some late nights with the British colonel commanding a detachment of Green Jackets as part of the military policing of the ceasefire. Gins and tonics on a covered veranda as the rain thundered down and lightning flashed. It didn't matter who asked it first. One of us always asked it. "We going to make this through?" London really had no idea how touch and go it was, how terribly improvised and simply lucky both the civilian observation and the military monitoring were. History will say it was a clean exercise and a clean result. In a way that's quite enough. No one understands the emotional detailing without personal experience. That's why so many soldiers won't speak about their experiences except to other soldiers. Silence is not post-traumatic stress. It's respect for condensed moments, compressed moments, when everything broadens into the possible while sucking down to the most elemental. That finger is twitching. Will he squeeze the trigger? So much surge of adrenaline suddenly compressed into a single question.

The various commanders accepted me into their midst. When, finally, it was almost all over, the election miraculously held but the results not yet announced, the two British colonels in Bulawayo hosted a reconciliation cocktail evening for their counterparts and other combatants. Halfway through the evening, a black guerrilla commander and a white helicopter pilot recognised each other. They both had had that moment of physical freeze while their minds raced through possibilities, including mathematical calculations of angles needed and time needed to wheel their weapon into place, and whether they could do it faster than the other, and then both simply hoping the other would not do it. The helicopter had hovered down to finish off the guerrilla unit. The guerrilla commander had survived the aerial assault. He willed himself to raise his AK47 and fire it into the cockpit. The helicopter officer was willing himself to turn his machine guns around and fire at the guerrilla. Their eyes met and neither fired. At the reconciliation reception, both recognised each other and fell into each other's arms. The British colonels motioned me to come outside with them. They couldn't be seen crying in public.

The nature of helicopters left a huge impression on me. I briefly was able to use one. A guerrilla colonel, Commander Ndlovu, whose units had been frequently attacked by them, asked to come up with me to see finally what his enemies saw. He had been trained in Moscow and had learned camp camouflage very well. He had not seen his wife for years. Here are three excerpts from a poem I tried to write in his voice.[12]

"Commander Ndlovu's Letter"

3.
Beloved, which flowers reach the heavens?
What water makes them over-reach themselves?
I write you this letter out of my tiredness.
I am encamped.
I am not in action.
I, like you, await announcements.
The well-spring of my heart is dammed, I think.

So, we all know about things that fall.
Little about things that rise.
If I look up, I am pierced.
Wounds fall out of the blue sky.

Wounds fall.
Today, a young observer came to the camp.
I asked for a ride in his helicopter.

The positions I had laid out
With cunning, with camouflage,
Were exposed totally.
I saw everything.
Sight rises into the air.
Destruction rains down.
I know now, in the great campaign,
They saw everything.
Sight alone rode with them.
Prayers, compassion,
                    Were not with them.

6.
In my dream, rose petals fell.
Sweet shrapnel.
Slowly, expressively, they traced directions
Across my body.
I lurched, turned, fell forward.
I awake.
There are no gunships in the sky.

8.
Beloved, this night, as on other nights,
I shall sit with British officers.
I eat their food.
They say, I read, that soon
I may sit, be as one
With those who fought me.
Against whom I fought.
Against whose violent flowers of death
Falling, cascading, irresistibly from the sky,
I resisted.
I, your absent husband.
I, Commander Ndlovu.
I write to you,
A stranger to his wife,
A stranger in his country.

When it was all over there were precious few celebrations. It was an "at last" moment, where the slow and violent trudge toward it had sapped all energy; and the long season of talks and negotiations in Lusaka and Lancaster House, followed by two months of tension as the peace miraculously held—but with worries every day that all could be lost and the world would be plunged into chaos—had taken the edge off any explosion of joy. I had invited the hotel workers to watch the official announcement on my television. They barely smiled, nodded their heads, and left. It was not just because the overwhelming victor, Mugabe, was not their man—Nkomo had been their kinsman—but because it had been so long in coming, and everyone knew things would not change overnight. But, for the visitors—observers, soldiers, diplomats, journalists—almost everyone I talked to reported that their arms shook for some minutes. A release of tension. The first colleague visitor I met was Ron Turton, part of the British administrative oversight team. He had been stationed in the southern town of Gwanda—a half horse town that was all the same a white supremacist stronghold. I had been challenged to a drinking match by white soldiers in its pub with huge photos of white Apartheid heroes. I held my own at the cost of a long weaving drive back to Bulawayo. The next time I came I brought my Nigerian Colonel colleague—in dress uniform—and had everyone stand to attention and salute him. It was a fitting revenge. I have lost contact with almost all my colleagues from that time. A brigadier with the same name as my Nigerian colonel, was later shot for plotting a coup. I never found out whether it was him. He or his namesake walked to the wall with a volume of poems by Byron.

"Suddenly His Arms Shake"

Suddenly his arms shake. Something
Grips him. Suddenly he feel weariness
Overwhelm him. He has seen Ron Turton
Who, like him, feels fulfilled but

Ashen with it all. Where now are Ron's
Jokes? To have Gwandad one's life away.
Legless in Gwanda. And the rest. And why
Are their arms shaking? Is the texture

Of historic moments like this slow fever?
Two men came here in search of history,
In search of justice, on behalf of dignity.

What has it come to? Trembling, they
Walk out. They are buying presents for
The return home. And this, this is
No longer their country.[13]

Leaving Zimbabwe after knowing something significant had happened, and knowing it was a formative experience for myself, did not diminish the need (and frankly, by now, the taste) for action. The feeling, as I said in the previous chapter, of leaving Uganda was very different. In Zimbabwe, there was something to play for—a hope, with some foundation, for the future. Uganda was bereft of almost all foundational structure and systems. If I had carried valises full of bank notes in Sri Lanka, it was a suitcase in Uganda. The desolation and devastation left by Amin was profound. Riding with Moabite was the least of my problems. For almost a month, I seemed to subsist almost entirely on bananas. There were even three grades of banana alcohol. Capturing a wild goat meant a speedy end to the unfortunate goat. For two decades afterward, I couldn't face eating another banana. But this mission too was meant to rebuild something. But the Ministry officials I was meant to be training in planning methodologies for the future were the ones who educated me with their tales of horror and constant fear of torture and execution. Their post-traumatic stress needed to be spoken. They, like me, had crossed the lines of untold factions of armies to reach the Mountains of the Moon. At the time, it all seemed a grand exercise in futility. I felt like a figure in an absurdist novel by Camus—absurd as defiant of futility, but futility still wins. At the same time, it felt like a magical realist novel. All reality had a missing core that left it floating in air refracting whatever legend anyone wished to put into it. A most literate country, I would pass bombed-out school buildings with graffiti still visible: "Things fall apart. The centre cannot hold." I excerpt my farewell poem here. [14]

"The Mountains of the Moon"

To leave Kampala
pass through a ring of steel
each boy carries a Kalashnikov
spare banana-shaped ammunition clips
respectful of our colours
unutterably polite

Sometimes I feel
the Chinese poet
middle-aged official
sent to distant provinces
our Landrover grinds
over shattered tarmac

The road where Amin's men
could not bear to fight
the proud Tanzanians
Swahili like Oxford English
Bore down

At Makasa marabou storks
wander in the ruins
they drop one face
behave like vultures
my companions say
they are perhaps
eagles
pelicans

I have wandered too long
in these countries
we cross the equator
clearly marked
I was born by ocean
I think of sea gods

In Kampala we stood
the Minister entered
the secretary brought three
settings for coffee
setting down tray
burned polish

I say arrowheads fly
strike flinty rock
no grass catches
generations later
horseman retrieves arrowhead
weeps for his ancestors
the sparseness
and economy
of their shots against the moon

"Swahili like Oxford English." I asked one of Amin's defeated soldiers how the Tanzanian army that finally evicted Amin from Uganda did it, why Amin's army stood and fought so little. On paper, the Ugandan army had so much more fire power. His answer was something that rang in me for years afterward. "They came upon us with language like Lords."

So, on mountaintop beneath the moon, I decided to use language and, as well as remaining in action, to write forever. I did not know how to express this when, at my interview at the University of Kent, they asked, "What is driving you, at this relatively late stage, to establish in this country an academic career?"

NOTES

1. Sun Tzu, *The Art of War*, Tokyo: Tuttle, 2008, from the 5th century BC.

2. Stephen Chan, *The Commonwealth in World Politics: A Study of International Action*, London: Lester Crook, 1988.

3. Roshan de Silva Wijeyeratne, *Nation, Constitutionalism, and Buddhism in Sri Lanka*, Abingdon: Routledge, 2014.

4. Luise S. White, *The Assassination of Herbert Chitepo: Texts and Politics in Zimbabwe*, Bloomington: Indiana University Press, 2003.

5. For a sympathetic view on Carrington's personal feelings throughout the entire process that followed, see John Newhouse, "Profiles—a Sense of Duty: Lord Carrington," *New Yorker*, 14 February 1983, and his own memoirs: Lord Carrington, *Reflect on Things Past*, London: Collins, 1988, chapter 13.

6. Michael Charlton, *The Last Colony in Africa: Diplomacy and the Independence of Rhodesia*, Oxford, UK: Blackwell, 1990, chapter 5.

7. Jeffrey Davidow, *A Peace in Southern Africa: The Lancaster House Conference on Rhodesia, 1979*, Boulder, CO: Westview, 1984.

8. The governor was Lord Soames. For his own recollections, see Lord Soames, "From Rhodesia to Zimbabwe," *International Affairs*, 56:3, 1980, pp 405–419.

9. Anthony Verrier, *The Road to Zimbabwe, 1890–1980*, London: Jonathan Cape, 1986.

10. Rajeshwar Dayal, "Zimbabwe's Long Road to Freedom," *Third World Quarterly*, 2:3, 1980, pp 466–486.

11. Stephen Chan, *The Commonwealth Observer Group in Zimbabwe: A Personal Memoir*, Gweru: Mambo, 1985.

12. From Stephen Chan, *Crimson Rain*, Lewston: Mellen, 1991, pp 5–13.

13. First published in Stephen Chan, *The Commonwealth Observer Group in Zimbabwe*, p 92.

14. From Stephen Chan, *Crimson Rain*, pp 30–31, of pp 30–35.

Chapter 3

Facing the Local

Today the sweeping views of Canterbury from any part of the campus have been built out. Universities have to expand to stay solvent. Higher education in the United Kingdom has not been a true public sector for decades. At the same time, government micro-management inhibits any actual market strategy, and makes business-planning a mere compensation for continual government shortfalls. The one recourse is to increase student numbers and, there being a finite number of UK students, this means overseas recruitment. For a time, the University of Kent had the most diverse student body in the country, with more than 120 nationalities represented. But the syllabus was staunchly Western and, to that extent, parochial.

All the same, the university occupied the highest point in a straight line across Europe until the Urals—so the joke was that the wind sweeping across the campus came straight from the Ural Mountains. But it was a beautiful, if wind-swept, campus with the hardiest roses outside Scotland, and lawns dotted with young people from well beyond the Urals. Difference, however, was not fully expected at faculty level. I arrived with my hair in spikes and wearing a leather biker's jacket. Professor Groom gently took me aside. I reverted to the guise I had adopted as a newspaper editor in New Zealand: dark suits, Cuban heels, open-necked silk shirts, and hair over my shoulders. It has stayed more or less like that ever since, the rise through faculty ranks being marked by gradually more expensive tailors.

At that time, 1987, Kent, along with LSE and Lancaster, housed the best Departments of International Relations in the United Kingdom. Kent was the stronghold of anti-realist pluralism, its subset of the paradigm being labeled World Society. It also had a distinguished niche in Track Two or informal diplomacy dedicated to conflict resolution. So I was going to do what John Groom told me to do and, as the hair grew long again, it became a feature flying in the wind as I strode in my dark suits across the campus. Doing as he advised involved publishing on a twin-track basis. The pressure to publish— for mine was not at first a permanent contract at Kent—had been eased while

I was in Oxford, occupying an office in Queen Elizabeth House that was far too grand for me, and acting as tutor to Chinese students who had been Red Guards in the Cultural Revolution, who had been "rehabilitated" in the countryside afterward, and who were now, older than normal students, allowed to go out to study. I was meant both to help teach them and understand their trauma. But, one day, shades of what happened at the University of Zambia, there was a knock on my office door and in walked Dr. Lester Crook, in between distinguished careers as an editor with Cassell and I. B. Tauris, and wanting for a while to be an independent publisher. "Do you have anything for me?" Well, yes, I had been meaning to write a short book both on the legal foundations of the Commonwealth Secretariat and how those allowed it to be an international actor under Shridath Ramphal. Working with Lester was done under a gentleman's agreement. There were no detailed contracts, merely an exchange of letters. Lester published the book,[1] and continued to publish much of my work when he joined I. B. Tauris. But this meant that within a year of my joining Kent, I had two scholarly books, as well as two other not-fully-scholarly books on African issues to my name—as well as two dozen papers in the academic and technical journals, all written either in Zambia or Oxford, and almost all deriving from my work criss-crossing Africa for the Commonwealth Secretariat. These gave me some cover to execute the twin-track in my own way.

But first, China once again exploded into view. This was the massacre of students in 1989 in Tiananmen Square—the square where Mao, after the Communist victory in 1949, the year of my birth, chanted an ancient dirge into a web microphone and claimed the Mandate of Heaven. In the square, forty years later, the students challenged that mandate and were crushed by tanks. I was appalled, not only because I supported the cause of democracy, and opposed slaughter by dictatorships, but also because of something simply Confucian: You may not kill your own children. On the night of the massacre, we followed the events by monitoring telephones and a fax machine. Such photos as the escapees could take were faxed out. The idea was to share. But the grainy photographs rapidly decomposed into dark illegible images as they were disseminated fax machine by fax machine. Even so, it was clear something horrific was happening. The next morning I wrote this poem.[2]

"Darkened Glasses"

He is walking his campus like the tearful cassiah
the photographs from Peking glued behind his
darkened glasses
He is muttering inconsequentials about mothers,
fathers, comrades

who have irretrievably grasped THEIR consequence
And he squints at the path beyond the
darkened photographs
does not, dares not look up
in case he embraces the mirages of hope
that sometimes dance in winds among the
clouds
He is walking his summer campus
A day for mourning, not for looking up
and blood is on the hands of his imagination
for he imagines something pure, revengeful
calculates not yet the path ahead
Behind him are walking generations
Ancestors
all the white
head-banded heroes of those who, unarmed
stood and fought and who, younger than he
are ancestors now
their footfalls behind, their photographs before
and they see certainly the path
and they say Arise
and the countless generations of ancestors behind
say Go Forward
Do Not Retreat
Die
It has been going on a very long time
this inability to look at the sky
and pluck a filament from the air that
Lights the Future
and the generations are themselves mourning
repeated failures
All of us
with the yellowed skin
red blood
and sun-struck eyes of antiquity.

The University of Kent accepted many escaped students on full scholar-ships. Some became my own students. At the same time, I began refusing offers to visit China, including invitations to accept prestigious visiting positions at such places as the national diplomatic academy. I refused until every single member of the Politburo at the time of the massacre had died or retired and was near death. Accepting these offers would have enhanced my career in the United Kingdom—they would have indicated international recognition—but it was going to have to be done the hard way, by grinding out the publications.

My first major work on Africa was a country-by-country analysis of militarized destabilization by Apartheid South Africa.[3] It remains still the only work to specify the often quite different methods South Africa used, depending on the country concerned. I had lived in Zambia for a key part of this period of destabilization, and had many friends in the Zambian high command. Where I lived was part of the safe-house network where ANC leaders would lodge their children when they had intelligence of a South African assassination raid. But my analysis was pretty much due to my study of strategy at King's. The hard times there paid off. But, in the interval between when I completed the book and when it appeared, momentous changes began occurring in the region. The beginnings of it did make it into the book, but the full denouement did not. That denouement began after the 1988 battle of Cuito Cuanavale in Southern Angola, when the South African army retreated in the face of Cuban military intervention and better generalship—although the South Africans bitterly contested this verdict; all the same, they retreated.[4]

In the wake of this, the hardliners in the Apartheid regime fell. Basically, it was the Cubans who changed the course of history here. An unknown moderate, F. W. De Klerk, became president of South Africa. He immediately held out an olive branch to the surrounding states his country had been bombing and devastating and, in 1989, he traveled to Zambia to have talks with President Kenneth Kaunda. The photos of their encounter are slightly comic—engaging, despite the severity of what was at stake. Holding their talks at Livingstone beside the Victoria Falls, what the local Tonga people call the *Musi o Tunya*, the Thundering Mist, there are pictures of Kaunda pointing things out to De Klerk—"Look, more water . . ."—as, just out of camera shot, their anxious aides held aloft umbrellas, I was trying to track this from Lusaka. I had friends and former students in both the Ministry of Foreign Affairs and the president's office itself.

"How did you brief the president?"

"We didn't. We had no file on De Klerk. No one thought this man would become president. In any case, the old man (Kaunda) never asked us for any briefing."

"My information from South Africa is that De Klerk devoured five-ring binders on Kaunda as part of his own briefing. You say our man is sailing blind?"

"Yes. He says God will guide him."

Amen to that. In fact, Kaunda, a veteran of negotiations, not least demonstrated at the 1979 Commonwealth summit in Lusaka, when the breakthrough over Rhodesia began, did brilliantly. It is officially denied to this day, but he told De Klerk he had to unban the ANC, and free Nelson Mandela. In early

1990, Mandela walked out of prison. Despite euphoria, four years of negotia-
tion lay ahead to achieve a political settlement. These negotiations were new
and hard for the representatives of the unbanned ANC. Many mistakes were
made along the way to the majority rule elections of 1994—but the one great
triumph was the world's finest constitution when it came to equal rights, not
just in racial terms, but across all terms of modern segregation—gender, sex-
ual orientation—everything is in there.[5] But the uneasiness of the negotiating
process meant that the academic boycott of South Africa remained in place.
I decided to break it and went to South Africa on the invitation of H. W. van
der Merwe—more on him in a succeeding chapter, for he played a role in the
very long process to free Mandela; De Klerk had a foundation from which
he could move. H. W., his initials, pronounced in Afrikaans as "Harvey," so
that Americans thought that was his name—in fact it was Hendrick—was
a Quaker conflict mediator of legendary stature. In the impoverished areas
of outer Cape Town, where gang war would alternate with protest against
the Apartheid regime, there were frequently standoffs between the township
dwellers and the armed police. H. W.'s conflict resolution process was to walk
into the middle of the forming battle lines and sit down. Then invite the lead-
ers of both sides to come and sit with him and parley. He was fearless. His
house in Observatory, a suburb near the university that held out against resi-
dential segregation for a very long time, was never locked. Everyone knew
that. No one ever stole anything from his house. He was known as the silent
man of God who was an honest broker. He was a confidant of both Kaunda
and Mandela, whom he would visit in prison. He was also stubborn, difficult,
and frustrating. But I loved H. W.: God's holy madman.

To understand the link between metropolitan Cape Town and the Salt
Flats—the shanties near the airport—I would get up at 5 a.m. and run for an
hour along the railway tracks that linked the two. Already at 5 a.m., still dark,
the carriages would be full of black commuters coming in for the long work-
ing day. And they were the lucky ones. One morning, showering after my run,
I took a telephone call. (H. W. had telephones in his bathrooms; it was that
kind of lifestyle.) The voice went, "Hello, I had a piece of paper thrust into
my hand as I was led away by the police. Your number was all there was on
it. I don't know why this number, but I was allowed only one phone call. My
family has no phone and I have no lawyer. So I rang the number on the piece
of paper." He was a coloured man from the impoverished outer township of
Atlantis, and he had been arrested for debt to a furniture store. South Africa
had not moved far from Charles Dickens's era. I dried myself off and found
H. W. His response was instant. "Well, it seems you and I are driving out to
Atlantis." He then added, "You're holding a visiting appointment in Geneva
right now too, aren't you? We're going to call you a professor of law from
Geneva." In fact, my appointment was indeed in the faculty of law in Geneva,

where for part of the year I had been flying in once a week to give a single
lecture on international relations and fly out again. We stretched the truth,
but it meant we sounded very impressive when we fetched up at the local
prison. The warden called out down the corridor, "Hey! You! A lawyer who
looks like Bruce Lee has come to get you out!" We posted his bail. Then H.
W. and I crashed into the office of the lawyer for the furniture store, and we
took turns bearding him as to how he could possibly apply Dickensian law,
and misuse so thoroughly his noble profession. Then we went to the furniture
store and paid off the debt. The poor recipient of the fruits of our adventure
was dumbfounded. It was a totally impoverished township. He deserved at
least a sofa on which his family could sit. But working with H. W. was fun. A
more serious mission awaited. For not everyone could afford a train ticket to
commute at 5 a.m., or any other time, to work in the city. You can see the Salt
Flats in the long distance from the high steps of the University of Cape Town.
It is a world to which no one goes. From the Salt Flats themselves, the view
of Table Mountain is not the picturesque tourist attraction. It is an obelisk of
foreboding and unattainable otherness.

With the unbanning of the ANC, people were swift to seek new alignments,
take sides. The perennial competitiveness among operators of small fleets
of mini-buses would now turn into open war between those who declared
themselves for the ANC, and those who were affiliated to gangs, and those
who were both, not to mention some small-scale private businesses. Whoever
controlled the routes into Cape Town was king. They were worth killing for.
A "taxi war" could be murderous.

There had been a taxi war just before my arrival. There was now meant to
be a truce. No one dared monitor the truce. The truce meant locking down the
fleets. Until the dispute was resolved, no one was going to drive into Cape
Town. There were rumours of violations, met with knives. H. W., who was
director of the University of Cape Town's Centre for Intergroup Studies—a
polite no-name for conflict resolution—was asked to provide a monitoring
report. "Um, Stephen, if you were provided with a driver and another pas-
senger looking bewildered beside the driver, would you do it?" Well, yes.
After all, the back seat passenger who was clearly a lost Japanese tourist,
whose driver had taken the wrong turning out of the airport, with his ever
snapping camera was simply an example of the idiocy of the oriental race. We
got H. W. his monitoring report. The fleets were parked in place. Stationary.
Photographic evidence. The truce was holding. No one was cheating. It took
a lot of inane oriental grinning out of car windows. Talks could begin.

On that visit, I flew from London to Johannesburg, thence to Cape Town,
so on the way back lingered in Johannesburg a few days—and took a trip to
the Voortrekker monument, the phallic cone that pays tribute to the Afrikaner
waggon trains that left Cape Town to colonise the interior. There is a hole

at the apex of the cone and, every year, on 16 December, a shaft of sunlight illuminates the Voortrekker code of belonging to South Africa—their South Africa. I wrote a poem about saboteurs seeking to explode the monument. It seemed a travesty that it was still there even as talks were underway to change the legacy of the Afrikaner colonization and subsequent subjugation of the country.

"There Is Blood Rising"

There is blood rising.
Blood rises.
In the long night
the stadium ablaze
cars fleeing Pretoria
someone has mined
the great monument
to the Voortrek
three cases of dynamite
could not bring it to the ground
but did some damage to its shape
and now, no longer obelisk-like
but crazily like a drunken ibis
it leans in the night
and this is enough
to raise the fire of joy
and raise the blood
to love the saboteurs
running, laughing, whooping
arms aloft
into the rural night
a case of dreams
clutched to their hearts
pumping rising
I tell you like three gods
laughing

I decided to go again in 1992. The ANC was faltering in the long negotiations. And, quite apart from the unsettled business of white political domination, not all was well between the ANC and the Zulu political mobilization of Inkatha. I accepted a visiting appointment at the University of Natal (now the University of KwaZulu-Natal), to be near the epicentre of Zulu-on-ANC slowly growing violence. Violence inside my own body was the opening shot as, in my small villa at the foot of the University of Natal campus, I felt the unmistakable start of my recurrent malaria—from an original infection some time before in Zambia. It was to be my welcoming party that night. I knew the stages—the freezing, the overheating, the convulsions—I thought I could get through them this time in seven hours. They were coming to pick me up in eight hours. Just. I was as white as my imagination of Edith Wharton. And weak. I told everyone I was jet-lagged and had also drunk too much on the plane. I sat and greeted everyone from my seat, and sipped tea all night long. Not the awful rooibos tea which is a South African favourite. They had been able to secure jasmine tea to ensure I felt as if I were really entering the dawn of a new multiculturalism. A Chinese professor was a distinct rarity at the University of Natal. One with shoulder-length hair and a BBC World Service accent made me exotic. Two hundred students signed up for my course. The class included for the first time a sizeable black intake, admitted as an early attempt toward equalization. Everyone had prophesied dire standards from them and the need for a lot of handholding. They were brilliant. But two episodes with them stood out for me.

By now the war against Apartheid was over. The negotiations had to succeed. There would be no return to armed rebellion if they failed. In my class were—but I had to find this out for myself, the university didn't seem to know, and there was no specialist psychological assistance available to them—youthful veterans of the ANC's armed wing who had been stationed in Angola. They had never seen action in South Africa itself, but had endured South African commando raids against them—specialist units crossing over from Namibia, until recently under Apartheid control, often taking a short cut through a narrow neck of Zambia, although this neck was fiercely contested by the Zambian army that was, all the same, short of intelligence as to when the South Africans would cross the inhospitable terrain of their territory. The commandos would show no mercy once they fell upon an ANC outpost. There was one white veteran of those raiding parties also in my class. Almost all semester he sat alone, not only in lectures but at the outdoor coffee bar after lectures. The ANC veterans would sit around a table, not far away, as a mutual-support unit. Each knew who the other was. I would sit, further away and watch. One day, just past midway in the semester, the white man got up from his lone table and, coffee in hand, walked over to the black table. Without a word—but I was breathless—they made room for him. Who knows what they discussed, whether they ever got around to the war—I doubt it, far too many atrocities—but peace is finally made through small talk and realising the other side is as capable of very bad jokes as oneself. Bad jokes is the one ingredient in conflict resolution that John Groom and H. W. had missed. Shameless bad humour, preferably over a drink—in South Africa, drinks around a braai, a barbeque—was very often the first step. And it allowed saving of face and sometimes the very slow overcoming of the fussy footnotes of discrimination. A braai is held outside. Provided you have an outdoors toilet facility, you need never invite your new black "friends" into your house. I forgave that but would count the number of braais it took before, finally, an invitation to dinner, inside, came. Then the black students would come to me and I would give them in private my Diplomatic Training seminar episode 39—I had recently trained the Ministry of Foreign Affairs of the new Eritrea—on knives, forks, wine, and French etiquette. I would say, "Look, they think they are very advanced in 'civilized' manners; a French person would think them still rough and provincial; I am teaching you to behave like French ambassadors; and only once should one of you utter the words, 'Ah, I see now some humour in Fanon's words, drawn almost certainly from Sartre's disquisition on absurdity and meaninglessness,' and then that person should immediately propose a toast to the absurdity of discrimination, make them all feel happy again and not perplexed, they won't have understood a word, and make the dinner easy."

It was a braai that settled the long-running standoff between the university's two karate clubs—one black and one white. I offered to teach the black club. And made sure the white club could see the "latest European fighting drills" I was teaching. Soon, the white president began greeting me with small talk. I preempted his request. "Look, not separately for your group, you do have fine standards but, all the same, perhaps a joint seminar to mark a new age?" His instant reply was expected by now, but still a breakthrough. "Perhaps we should hold a braai for everyone."

But I had come to look at something that could derail the whole project of a rainbow nation, and that was not white-on-black violence—for a while, many people would do their best with the tiny incremental stages of acceptance—but there was still the question of black-on-black violence. I had already taken to including the outskirts of Cato Manor in my running route. This was the impoverished slum community near the foot of the university hill. As with the University of Cape Town and the Salt Flats, there was no outreach at all—but Cato Manor was much closer to the university than the Salt Flats.

The hills of KwaZulu around Natal were becoming the sites of small scale but still deadly massacres. ANC villages would be attacked by Zulu Inkatha militias, anxious to ensure a cleansed KwaZulu in the final bargaining stakes with what seemed, negotiating mistakes and difficulties notwithstanding, some kind of ANC majority government. The ANC was for the most part not their party. The militias borrowed directly from Shaka's tactics: an envelopment shaped like a bull's horns; the bull's horns were open at the top to allow some survivors to flee and spread word of terror and encourage others to depart; the cradle of the horns was populated by female militia members, whose job was to loot; traditional Zulu weapons were used to avoid blue-on-blue crossfire casualties from opposite sides of the horn formation, but this meant that people in between were beaten to death. It was impossible to write an academic paper about this. And certainly not at the time, as optimism had to be built toward a momentous change at least of some sort. And, to be fair, since I have been very critical of him,[6] the ANC's Jacob Zuma, himself a Zulu, was put to good use as a mediator to dampen down the conflict. But I did write a very long poem. It wasn't published till some years later and, only then, at the request of Roland Bleiker, the special issue editor of *Alternatives*, an International Relations journal having the rare kind of creative moment only Roland could bring.[7] I'm sure no one in my profession had the slightest clue what the poem meant.

"Body Count in Natal"

I
The Buddha asked his disciples to wander to
be not at home to worldly things
to not love the merely familiar.
But under the full moon of Durban running for
the full balloons of my lungs and seeing light
shine on ocean
I am his rebel disciple
familiar to the disjunctions of the world
how death also runs along the moonlit coast and
the sunsets of the eastern sea
red like a doctor's scarlet robes are
because the horses of the sky are
slain by infamies and torchlit on the
pyres of heaven.

II
His hair over his face he has planned the phoenix tattoo for the left
side of his back
its tail become the Miro painting of
his disciple dreams
not a possession on a white home wall but a
skin he grows into
and cannot see.

For years he has dreamt that secret skin
hoping the Buddha might permit this dream behind him conscious
of it like a scar
man-made, man-coloured, but with a tail like
newborn heaven
and forgive him.

Forgive his dream of home
nothing skinned in the picture frames
a vast library with that final book collected
to outweigh by cover-closed words
that heavily inked, heavenly inked
portrait of the slaughtered horses of the sky.

Teacher, one by one we come to you
lifetime by lifetime we approach some sight of you.

How many lifetimes did they die like sheep
In the purple tinged hills of Natal
Each one thinking in cudgel-loosened blood
That they were really horses of the sun?

This doctrine, Teacher, the disciple also
wishes to change.

For days he has sat in a broad hotel
writing an epistle to his teacher
composing it also as he runs

"Winged horses like phoenixes rise
the burnt blood lands like phoenixes rise
hidden, if need be, from the teaching angels' eyes

and his wanderings are a video soon
far from familiar in a familiar room
and his exhale is a storm
that rinses the red-splattered moon."

III
Because rain has fallen heavily and broken
nine years of drought and imported food
coarse grains, wrong-grown, too moist
for the dry stomachs of sun's castaway offspring

he drinks water hourly and pisses it hourly
heaven's tube and his only work that is blessed
is to piss water coloured like sun
and this too is familiar, the attenuation of hopes

and if only it had rained these years
as often as he's pissed

so that in the broad plains he might not have smelt
the dryness with its brief stale irrigations.

* * *

The trick is, they'd say, to declare independence *from*
heaven and its sunset horses
to rise above, not merely rebel, not rise against.

To be a warrior requires even greater preparation than
a priestly disciple's.
The koans are lighter than a sword
a scabbard fuller than a scripture

A Buddha is invulnerable.
Shall I run the northern seaboard
to repay in blood all Natal's leached life? Echo on
earth the snorting evening colours?

African soil is red like rust
every drenched blade made a compost continent every
prayer cannot charm it away
in the white room there is shelter
green-laden trees hide the heavens
let colour-free moisture slide on my panes.

IV
When the horses of the sun ran they were like
the horses of Greek Achilles and the same Greek form was given
the young representations of Buddha
and the Hellenic sense of blood mixed with
the Indian sense of blood and this much at least
is primeval and common. Kill my sister
and I shall flush your cisterns with raw red.

The middle way of Siddartha was to abjure revenge to
abandon love's desire
to deem them inessential,
the passionless way
no stumbling cross-laden haul to eternity here
was a navigation through extremities,
but whose extremities?
the Buddha cut Asia like a knife.

Thus cleaved, if factionally alive, the heart
was given over to sadness for the world
bruised in a middle way
exuding medium love for the poor and dying
the disciples gathering alms in competition
with the lepers.

Listen, what we have now in the west
is the re-Hellenicised conscience-bearing teacher
whose horses run like the sun
and whose lack of solidity gives us every excuse
to be neither too left nor too right
But in Africa the horses of the sun trample marrow
to reach their sunset slaughter
and the mourning of night
gives way to the sight-filled horrors of dawn
and reincarnated horses file mockingly
into the blue skies of Natal, east to west
sureties engraved on Tibetan bridles,
silver simple mandalas.

V
98 dead over Easter
that's the count by third day's evening
enough to compensate stallions of the chariot
except that horses are not what the attackers
have in mind
not horses but bulls
a bull's horn to be exact
horns of a dilemma they laugh
as they sweep in

and that's why the traditional weapons
AKs produce too much crossfire
The opposite horn could be slaughtered too
but in the recipe of Shaka
an enclosure that bludgeons to death,
with horn's cradle
politically correct
the women sweeping in behind
to loot all made unowned

At least that Other who rose once
allowed an ear to be struck off
before the doctrine of surrender

Enter a slaughtered village
furniture, limbs, eyes, penises gone
not an ear lies straining in the silence.

My eyes ache from the sunsets
my friends gather up pieces
relatives will have some semblance of
completed shape in body bags
I am gasping from the stench of heaven's irrigation
And proving my discipleship
I am in a corner vomiting blood

VI
The disciple who knows where to buy
all the morning papers tonight
in every city on earth
who has monitored the killing fields of battle
but pales at the sites
of defenceless slaughter
who has rid horses in the mountains of Africa
and stared unglassed at yellow light
who, besuited, hair slung back
is the convincing visitor
seen entering and leaving hotels
is the disciple who starts a new sect.

You may fight back.
You may fight.
You may sacrifice your own horse.
You may invent the ritual.
You may interpret the scripture.

But do it without hate.
For murder too there is also that calm middle way.

VII
When he comes home
a weight lifts from his head
a virtual reality helmet fades to memory
the memory is edited
he was strong and vomited nothing
the horses of the sun become a metaphor
the phoenix is glimpsed when he arranges
the wardrobe mirrors
his hair is sleek in no dust-laden storm

he attends his students' graduations
in unthinking black and red
he becomes middle-class for the sake of his life
and he sings a broad song in streets
full of light.
Winged horses like phoenixes rise
the burnt blood lands like phoenixes rise
written, if need be, through editing eyes

and his wanderings are a video soon
which seems unfamiliar in a white-washed room
and his night sigh's a storm
that rinses a dream-splattered moon.

It soon became time to leave at the end of the semester. I was invited to my final party in Durban. It was held in an enclosed courtyard. There was an ornamental pool, columns supporting the covered seating area surrounding the pool, discreet lighting that simulated candles. In this room, apart from me and the waiters, there were only thirty people. For once, the South African Chablis lived up to its reputation. Halfway through the evening, the host came up to me and said, "If a bomb went off now, the entire white resistance of Durban would be wiped out." I said, "Entire? There are thirty here." "Yes, many people made noise. These are the only ones who took risks, who broke the law, helped the underground." I was stunned. There had been books about how small this minority was in the various cities where white liberals purported to make a stand.[8] And, to be fair, the making of noise did help stir international objection to Apartheid. All the same, risk is risk—by that I mean risk of imprisonment or harm—and few took that risk. The late afternoon of my departure, two of the guests at this party took me for drinks in a waterfront bar. Even now, their real names should remain hidden.

"The People's Representatives Prepare to Bed Down for the Night"

For all I know Ian and Jan
are still at the Victoria
drunk by now with Kai
all three replete with seafoods
and Ian's stories of Moscow.
For all I know: aloft again
five hours out of Durban
away from Ian's dilemma of faith
as he and Kai discuss the revolution
and Jan ponders the profit
on antiques and upland native

crafts.
Laid alongside the images of ebony
bedsteads
the AKs of the oft-dreamt uprising
the Winter Palace stormed on beaches
seafronts
in shanties several million strong
in the Victoria
fed on mussels and kalamari
three soldiers of the enchanted dream.
Ordering their coffees at last
another day without instructions
another night with rifles
dreamily sequestered under pillows
and perhaps one thought
of Stephen thundering back to London
carrying with him rains
and a critique that longs.
It is so long in its longing
my comrades.

I would return often to South Africa, as well as many other African locations. But, first, there was the other side of the twin-track. Affronted by the realism of the United States, in which power was the major if not sole determinant of direction in world politics, John Groom had long sought to organize a European counter-base for the academic discipline of International Relations. Europe, after all, had suffered the depredations of power in World War II and now saw the value of pluralism, of European organization and cooperation as an alternative, if not an antidote to power. He persuaded the European Consortium for Political research to host special sessions on International Relations. I returned in 1992 to the first big event. It was to be in Heidelberg. All I knew about Heidelberg was the film of the Sigmund Romberg operetta, *The Student Prince*, with the voice of Mario Lanza lip-synched by the more handsome Edmund Purdom. We had already had to sing *Gaudeamus igitur* at graduations, but the reason why I knew the operetta had been my father's liking for the students' drinking song. My parents were still alive. I was made to promise I would stand on a table and sing that song, just like in the film. As it turned out, I did—but only with the permission and indulgence of the university rector, whose guest I was one night. In his reception room, I explained that I was Chinese and therefore filial. He let me do it. But Heidelberg was very beautiful. Walking along the banks of the Neckar River every morning, looking up the hills to Goethe's walking route, was wonderful. And it was autumn. Red burned everywhere and it was more magical than any film. But of 600 papers presented at the conference, only two were on non-Western themes, non-American and non-European themes. Mine and that by James Piscatori, the renowned scholar of Islamic politics.[9] We were quarantined into a single session where we both presented. Given at least the importance of Islam in the world today—only nine years later, 9/11 would explode upon New York—it was an amazing short-sightedness in 1992 to have only one paper on things Islamic. But luminaries from the profession, like James Rosenau, came to our session. Piscatori and I knew we had made a small breakthrough. The next big ECPR Special Sessions conference was scheduled for Paris in 1995. I thought I could ramp up what James Piscatori and I had begun. By now, I had an ally, Osmo Apunen, and had taught in his summer schools at the University of Tampere in Finland. I asked John Groom how many sessions I could have in Paris. He said the maximum for any one convenor was four. The host *Institut d'etudes politiques* or *SciencesPo* did not have a surfeit of rooms. I told Osmo. He rang the Finnish Embassy. They let us use their premises. We put on seven sessions. The result was a book that established the possibility of a new way forward for International Relations.[10]

Not that any of this helped my promotion prospects. I had by now published more books than most full professors. But they were "strange" books. It was useless to moan, and moaning is quite alien to me. The schoolboy who sometimes opened his lunchbox to find sandwiches without filling, and dinner that night being last night's burnt rice scraped off the side of the pot, understood the family was in dire straits and never moaned. I offered to deploy my managerial skills. The history of those at least was undeniable. I had helped ministries and governments come into existence after war and revolution—of that, more in the next chapter. So, in 1994, I accepted the chance to become director of the University of Kent's London Centre for International Relations. This was a graduate school of just shy of 100 students in rented rooms from the London School of Economics. It was making a loss and needed turning around. This was duly done, as well as garnering more distinctions in the MA degree than what was achieved in my department in Canterbury. In 1996, I took a call from the vice-chancellor of Nottingham Trent University, only promoted to full university status four years earlier. It had superb professional faculties—engineering, fine art and design, and law, in particular. He said he wanted to have at least one flagship purely academic faculty. Would I contemplate applying for the first externally recruited dean of humanities position? He added he would double my salary. Kent immediately offered me a full professorship—but there is a timeline for appreciation, and it leads to departure. My new vice-chancellor asked whether I could achieve even one or two top scores in the United Kingdom's research assessment exercise, an artificial but ferocious national adjudication of the worth of published research. I said yes, but I wanted a treasury. I was going to buy in star researchers like a football manager buys in star strikers. I modeled my deanery on Jose Mourinho, then making waves at Chelsea. I fast-tracked the younger faculty if they showed the least talent in publishing. Squeezed top and bottom, the middle-ranking faculty responded with elan. They always could do it. They just needed someone to say they could. I got the vice-chancellor two top scores. I was then the only Chinese dean of humanities in Europe. If I was Chinese I was meant to do engineering or business schools. The head-hunters started calling. I instead applied in 2002 for the post of foundation dean of law and social sciences at the School of Oriental and African Studies. And was amazed I was appointed. It is a vexatious but wonderful institution, my academic work flowered being finally among like-minded colleagues, but leading and managing them was like making cats march pass like the Coldstream Guards. And, to this day, there has never been enough money.

At least the academic discipline of international relations was slowly changing. My former head of department at the University of Natal, Mervyn Frost, was appointed to Kent. He was the first (and only) disciplinary colleague to understand my poem about the horses of the sun. He added dimension to Kent's project of anti-realist pluralism. We had already, while I was in Natal, debated his own project of establishing a communitarianism as an inevitable overarching norm in the world.[11] I said it couldn't be done unless the ingredients of what he called "settled" moral positions could encompass the different methodologies that different cultures used to consider them moral. The end result was deceptive without appreciating the intellectual and methodological genealogies that wrought the end result. We still differ on this, but finally a debate was possible. Mervyn was not someone included among those who took risks of physical harm and loss of liberty in the fight against Apartheid. He was not at the party of thirty. But every night for years, he had turned a blind eye to his office photo copier being used to churn out thousands of leaflets that mobilised opinion against the system, and leaflets that supported the outlawed ANC. His stationery and ink bills must have been horrendous. Sometimes it is a settled norm to see no "evil" in order to fight against evil. This minor contradiction could be writ large in the world's myriad approaches to what was right. At SOAS, there was no equivocation about such things. There were myriad approaches. End of story. But there were never working budgets and, more than once, there was almost an end to the SOAS story. Despite its small size, it competes with Kent in terms of diversity—129 student nationalities is a norm, but its faculty is also more diverse than any other in the United Kingdom. Its campus doesn't have sweeping views of Canterbury, looking beyond the horizon to the far-off Urals. It is in polite Bloomsbury, where the thinking of Fabianism, British social democracy, British foreign aid, Keynesian economics, and individualistic feminism began. The times may now demand more radical solutions, but a grand internationalism still emanates from this square in London.

NOTES

1. Stephen Chan, *The Commonwealth in World Politics: A Study of International Action 1965 to 1985*, London: Lester Crook, 1988.

2. This was never published in any traditional fashion but was read on social media platforms on the anniversary of the slaughter by British actor Duncan Patrick Woodruff.

3. Stephen Chan, *Exporting Apartheid: Foreign Policies in Southern Africa, 1978–1988*, London: Macmillan, 1990.

4. For my latest assessment of this, see Stephen Chan, "Fidel Castro and the Moment of Change in Africa," in Sabella Abidde and Charity Manyeruke (eds.), *Fidel Castro and Africa's Liberation*, Lanham, MD: Lexington, 2020, chapter 3.

5. Rob Amato, *Understanding the New Constitution*, Cape Town: Struik, 1994.

6. Stephen Chan, *Southern Africa: Old Treacheries and New Deceits*, New Haven, CT: Yale University Press, 2011, chapter 9.

7. Stephen Chan, "Body Count in Natal," *Alternatives*, 25:3, 2000, pp 323–328.

8. For example, Paul B. Rich, *White Power and the Liberal Conscience: Racial Segregation and South African Liberalism, 1921–60*, Manchester, UK: Manchester University Press, 1984.

9. James P. Piscatori, *Islam in a World of Nation-States*, Cambridge, UK: Cambridge University Press, 1986.

10. Stephen Chan, Peter Mandaville, and Roland Bleiker (eds.), *The Zen of International Relations: IR Theory from East to West*, Houndmills, UK: Palgrave, 2001.

11. Mervyn Frost, *Towards a Normative Theory of International Relations*, Cambridge, UK: Cambridge University Press, 1986.

Chapter 4

Facing the Contradictions

MEETING H. W.

In 1984, Lusaka was a destitute place. Nothing worked. Officially, every-thing had been sacrificed to resist white rule in Rhodesia. But Zimbabwe had finally achieved independence in 1980. This certainly didn't mean an end to South African destabilization of Zambia and all neighbouring countries. But people were beginning to feel frustration at obvious government ineptitudes in economic planning. I myself contrived a data set for one of the ministries so it would have something to present during a meeting with the IMF. No one had kept data. It was a case of inventing the plausible. I think the IMF recognised that everything was a contrivance but was more concerned with a macro picture where economic recovery seemed a distant dream. What the micro picture meant in terms even of supposed middle class living was epito-mised by university housing. Handsome terrace townhouses went for hours without water, sometimes electricity. When the water came on you filled the bath. If you bathed, you didn't release the dirty water. It was kept to flush the toilet. If there was anything left, it watered the garden. I landscaped the patio garden. With pilfered bricks I laid down a walkway shaped like a giant question mark. I re-read the French existentialist works on absurdity. There were no telephones. In the entire University of Zambia, there were working telephones only in the vice-chancellor's office. One day a breathless mes-senger came to my office. I had chosen the highest point in the university, as much to be left alone as for the view. I had a great terrace and a view of what remained a manicured campus. The messenger panted that there was an urgent call from London for me.

The call explained that a two-person delegation, an unofficial delegation, would arrive in Lusaka from South Africa the next day. They were coming to talk to the ANC. They were very nervous—in fact, as it turned out, only one of the two was—so, as their icebreaker, could I host them for dinner on their first night before their meetings with the ANC the next morning? I agreed, for clearly the real ice being broken was that the visit was happening at all. Unofficial, or Track Two Diplomacy, utilizing people from nongovernmental sectors—deniable, but reporting directly to official quarters—was being used to begin negotiations between the Apartheid regime and its chief opponents. It became in fact one side of a twin-track approach by Pretoria. The other side was to increase military incursions under a strategic doctrine called Total Strategy. More than once, we took in the children of ANC families going into hiding because ANC intelligence signalled an impending assassination raid by South African commandos. The families split into fragments. At least the children would escape if their parents went down. These raids did not worry about collateral damage. Everything in the specified target house would be shot to pieces.

But my chief concern was, "Dinner . . . will I have water? Will I have electricity for the stove? How will I create the right impression?" I invited two Zambian students to the dinner. They intuited at once the nature of the occasion.

The townhouse was frescoed by my own murals, gallant but futile efforts to reduce the color scheme of the university's effort to redecorate but using the only color paint it had. And it had that because that was all that could be had. My murals owed much to paint from the black market. They were horizons—beyond which were other worlds. The melancholy gaze at far horizons was what kept people psychologically stable in the face of national penury, unavailability of basic facilities and even food, and a national currency that increasingly bought nothing of actual value. Into this milieu, H. W. van der Merwe, of whom I wrote in the last chapter, and Piet Muller, wandered—Piet dazed and confused. The water lasted, and the electricity held. The scent from the jasmine trellis made it all seem exotic. My dinner was passable. Afterward, the students having departed, and while I was washing the dishes—"while the water lasts," I explained—Piet came almost dashing up to me in the kitchen. "Stephen, that was amazing." I was about to say he didn't need to be kind about my cooking, but he said: "That was the first time I have ever dined with black people!" I daresay probably the first time with a Chinese person too. But my students were first class intellects. One went on to complete a doctorate at Oxford. And, as I say, they "knew" they were there, in the most subtle manner, to prove as elegantly as possible a simple point. I almost said, but didn't, "and they knew how to use their knives and forks and sip properly the contraband Californian wine."

H. W. had been to Lusaka before, and had gained the confidence of President Kaunda. His bringing of Piet was the breakthrough. Piet was a hugely influential editor of the Apartheid-supporting right-wing newspaper

Beeld. And came from very high political family with position in the government apparatus. He was hardly Track Two in any disinterested sense, but his report back, above all, was going to be the key. H. W. didn't give details about this and other trips to Lusaka until his 2000 autobiography[1]—with an appreciative foreword by Nelson Mandela—but Piet produced reports and published some newspaper articles suggesting that dialogue with the ANC was possible;[2] although, given his readership, the interpretation of what he said might well have been that, Oh My God, they're not barbarians and have actual table manners.

The trip basically set up a long series of Track Two encounters that, if nothing else, provided some basic confidence building for South Africa—for they all involved highly placed persons pretending not to be—and, for the ANC, some practice for the Track One negotiations to come. All the while, from 1984 to 1988, as I have described earlier, Pretoria was bombing the surrounding countries, sponsoring and supporting rebel movements, in the case of Angola sending in its own army and, in the case of Mozambique, almost certainly assassinating President Samora Machel (no one else would have had the technological know-how to re-set homing beacons to direct Machel's plane into a mountain).[3]

But, when it was all over, I went in 1990 to visit Piet in Pretoria. He greeted me warmly. But the walk down the main street to his newspaper office was a spectacle—although I certainly did not plan it that way. I was dressed as I normally dressed at the University of Kent: long hair, a white silk shirt, a dark blue suit, black leather urban cowboy boots with Cuban heels (they were fashionable then). Cars screamed and skidded to halts in the street. People craned out of windows. Clearly, difference was not much seen in the streets of Pretoria and, indeed, no one in all of South Africa, as far as I could tell, dressed like a refugee from *GQ* magazine. The capital city was starkly provincial. But, on that trip, after I left H. W.'s house, I also went to the campuses of the Universities of Stellenbosch and Pretoria. The students, all white, stared also. I went to the Stellenbosch Department of Political and Administrative Studies and knocked on the doors of professors to introduce myself. Stunned silence as I left my calling card behind. I just remember thinking that this would take a long time.

But, before then, back in Lusaka shortly after H. W. and Piet's visit, I received other visitors. They were from SWAPO (South West Africa People's Organisation), the liberation group, like the ANC exiled in Lusaka, fighting for majority rule in South African-governed South West Africa (now Namibia). They depended greatly on foreign aid. After greetings, their opening line was:

"The Swedish auditors are arriving in Lusaka tomorrow."

"That's nice."

"Um, we seem to have, er, misplaced some of the money they gave us . . ."

"Yessss, misplacement is, er, quite understandable . . . you are afraid they will call it maladministration or even misappropriation?"

"Yes."

"What can I do for you?"

"Well, um, if we go to the casino tonight, and we stake you, could you win that amount back for us? The accounts could then be squared with money in hand. Um, the sum is quite a lot . . . ah, could you . . .?"

Well, it was a world of racial stereotypes, this much a legacy of Apartheid, and Chinese are meant to be lucky . . . so we went that night to the only casino in town, on the top floor of the Intercontinental Hotel, where Thabo Mbeki used to stay on his visits to Lusaka when not directing the international ANC. Thankfully, Thabo was not in town. What was about to happen was ridiculous.

For an hour, dressed in a blue safari suit from Simpsons in Piccadilly, expensive cocktail in hand (this adding to the SWAPO debt), impervious to the view of Lusaka below, I watched the roulette table. You can minimise your losses (and gains) by betting small amounts on the colors—red or green—there are lots of reds and greens. Or you can play the numbers. Each number is different. After an hour I had attained a Zen state. I walked to the table and bet everything on a high number. It won. I handed the winnings to my SWAPO minders and said, "Don't misplace this until after the auditors have gone." I have never played roulette since. You can, once in your life, decipher the wheel of God like an epiphany. It will never happen again. But it brought home to me the tragic realization that the struggle for liberation can be as much farce as valour and sacrifice. Thus, by farce, I contributed to Namibia's eventual independence. I hoped those who paid huge sacrifices could forgive me.

Somehow—but Lusaka, for all its worldliness in terms of liberation groups based there, was a small town—I became known as a "go-to" person. If not farce, it could bring me face-to-face with tragedy. In 1984, the Ethiopian famine in full swing, Israel was internationally castigated for airlifting only Falasha Jews out of the famine zones. One day, seated on my patio, a gentleman approached. I had known him from a distance but, without too much ceremony, he identified himself as perhaps speaking for Mossad, the Israeli intelligence agency. "We are unable any more to evacuate the Falashas from Ethiopia. We are going to smuggle them across the border to Sudan. Planes will be waiting there to bring them to Israel. The Sudanese Government, after some inducement, will not know. The border guards will be bribed. All the same, to keep it all deniable we need non-Israelis to ride shotgun for the convoys. We know you as a reliable operative in righteous operations. Would you . . .?"

I declined. But, ever after, struggled within myself. At the day of judgement, and I am asked, "Did you save anyone during the Ethiopian famine?" and I say, "No," what could I answer to the follow-up question: "Did you have an opportunity to save anyone?" I did, and I declined on the grounds that it was selective. But, if save some against save none, even if selective, the question becomes more technical—like a doctor's in a war zone. "What reasoning did you deploy in your *triage*? When you gave medicine to some and let others die?" Others die. All of these stories are backdropped by the inevitable realization that, in every single theater, others died. This became the deep sorrow of my most committed offerings to Africa, and my single greatest failure in living the international. Good friends died, and I could do nothing at all to save them.

In the end I had to move house often in Lusaka. I brooded much on the last of my patios.

"A Day in Lusaka"

Sometimes a deep melancholy seizes him.
He knows this because he becomes more gallant.
Though—what gallantry has to do with his work today—
sitting in the sun, fending off mosquitos, still reading Sartre—
is beyond even educated guesses.

Sits, in a deck chair, of course on a deck,
a house in the Spanish style, all arches.
Street's full of them. Could be in any suburb.
Any part of the world. Irredeemably bourgeois,
he adds up his deficits, convinces himself he leads
a glad spartan life (if only it weren't for the mosquitos).

There are pictures that have always fuelled his imagination.
Regis Debray and his Spanish wife contemplating the Seine.
Sartre assisted by Glucksmann at a conference on refugees.
Another picture: Sartre greets Aron after many years.
Glucksmann, younger, obscured, head bowed, wears
a beatific smile. For him, the world was reconciled.

Ah, how sentimental Africa has made him. His melancholy
stems from that. He'd like to help old partners
find each other one more time. He'd like to make love
(a mosquito coil aflame in the corner). Invite
all female visitors to his room. Discuss philosophy,
how we are changed, if not saved, and postulate,

in place of cigarettes, after each orgasm, whether angels
study in Paris, grow up in Dacca or Lusaka,
obscure questions, gallantly phrased, free, unalienated,
unreconciled. [4]

THE TEMPERING OF VICTORY

The memory of how Track II diplomacy could be used, both with good results
and more ambivalent ones, but always deniably if things got embarrassing,
was fresh in my memory. And, unlike many of Track II's acolytes, I saw how
it could be used cynically—if problematically beneficially—as in the case of
the approach by Mossad.

I was a member of the University of Kent when, in 1991, the Stalinist dic-
tatorship of Mengistu in Ethiopia, even though supported by military advisers
from the Soviet Union, fell to rebel forces. Two rebel armies had combined.
One came from the coastal region we now know as Eritrea, and their price
for contributing to victory was independence from Ethiopia. But the Eritreans
had absolutely no government experience or apparatus. They had fought
for thirty years, going up into the mountains when Jimi Hendrix was at his
height. They grew their hair like his. They wired their zithers, what Coleridge
called dulcimers, to generators and amplifiers and in the wilderness rescored
all their songs to incorporate the wah wah note bends and distortions of "All
along the Watchtower." It was awful and wonderful.

My colleague at the University of Kent, Hazel Smith, a long-time sup-
porter of the Eritrean cause, had hoped to be helpful to the construction of a
new government. When circumstances made this difficult, I said I would try.
I was also spurred by anger. UNITAR (United Nations Institute for Training
and Research) had offered to train the unborn Eritrean foreign service—for
what I thought was a phenomenal sum—hoping a foreign donor would pick
up the tab and also, at a stroke, solve the then financial problems of UNITAR.
I didn't think it was proper to profit from so many years of struggle. I rang the
Foreign and Commonwealth Office. "Stake me seed money from your discre-
tionary budget. I can do this for £6000. I'll put together a training programme
at a fraction of the cost UNITAR is proposing. You can take all the credit." It
was a Track II intervention, working with the full knowledge of Track I, but
proposed by Track II. I wanted to design something without being just used
by someone.

I probably also wanted to redeem my decision in 1984 not to help.

I proposed to do it on a shuttle basis: small teams flying in, teaching inten-
sively for a week, leaving behind "homework," with another team flying in a
month or so later. In the end we did this from 1993 to 1997, utilising retired

ambassadors as well as senior academics with experience in applied international relations. The first ambassador we persuaded to come on board was the legendary Sir Harold Walker (Hooky), who had been UK ambassador to Iraq as Gulf War One began and the Western hostage crisis erupted. In fact, it was Hooky who negotiated behind the scenes the release of the hostages—although credit, as it is wont to go, went to the high-profile political figures seen pontificating righteously on nightly television. Hooky would be seen in daily interviews from location, basically urging patience and restraint—always shaved and suited, despite his embassy's water having been turned off and essentially placed under siege by the Iraqis. His necktie tied always perfectly in a correct Windsor knot. But he had also been ambassador to Ethiopia and spoke at least one of the regional languages fluently. He and I were the first team to embark to Asmara, transiting through Addis Ababa in Ethiopia. Hooky was late getting to Heathrow. It was only twelve days after his hip operation. I couldn't tell. He bounded all over the place.

But he brought gravitas and wit to the occasion. It was a two-person team of contrasts, and this worked very well. We were housed in the Embasoira Hotel. It's still there and the tourist photos suggest it has been renovated, though reviews suggest it is barely above desperate.[5] It was certainly very desperate then. Everyone tried their best and I would be up at 6 a.m. each morning to see, several floors down below my balcony, a tanker come; and the driver would lift a flagstone in the carpark and fill the underground tank with water. UN observers who had never been far from Manhattan before, sent to report on the national plebiscite for independence from Ethiopia—as agreed with the new Ethiopian government—complained to me that the hotel had no hot water. I told them that no other hotel had water at all. This was being done just for us. These observers were there because the more senior UN personnel were conducting elections in Cambodia, and I had declined an invitation to go there myself. No one was expecting trouble with the plebiscite. Its outcome—a vote for independence—was a foregone conclusion. I watched the voting stations manned by school children—because they were a guarantee of officials who could read and write.

The hotel was a short stroll from downtown Asmara—which was basically one street with a modest cathedral, Our Lady of the Rosary, a legacy of Italy's presence in the past. Of the stubborn Italian effort to colonise Ethiopia, unable ever to be more than fleetingly and never totally successful, only Eritrea could be said to have received a proper Italian imprint. Amazingly, in a city recovering from war, ice cream and shoes were made in the Italian fashion. I stocked up on shoes. Everybody in the United Kingdom thought I had returned from Naples. But the town was dusty and undeveloped. Walking down the main street I was adopted by youngsters. One said, "Only the masters can wear hair like that." I thought he meant a kung fu master as he must have seen in the Grade Z movies that would have come even to Asmara. In fact, he meant that social regimentation was already setting in, and only a member of the elite would have the freedom to look like me.

The future diplomats of the country, the personnel of the new Ministry of Foreign Affairs, were by and large a ragged, if sometimes brilliant, bunch. These were the people who adapted Jimi Hendrix's electronics in the mountains, who (with the help of a New Zealand doctor, Fred Hollows,[6] often claimed by the Australians) manufactured inter-ocular lenses in their field hospitals for their wounded, and calculated artillery trajectories by doing the mathematics with ballpoint pens on the backs of their hands. And my old friend, Mary Sinclair, during the 1984 famine, had delivered a shipload of New Zealand aid to Eritrea.[7] When the ragged future diplomats heard I was born in New Zealand, they were elated. But they had fought a long war of sometimes appalling brutality. They had developed ways of looking at the world. As I was beginning my lectures to them, we received word that an IMF delegation would arrive in town the next week. So, I thought I had better begin by a lecture on how to negotiate with the IMF. A former fighter, his hair still in major Hendrix style, put up his hand and simply said, "But, Stephen, if the IMF are like that, when they come to town why don't we just shoot them?" News of that would have been welcomed in many African capitals, but I realised we had a very long way to go before they would become a proper Ministry of Foreign Affairs. As it was, Eritrea declined to borrow any funds from the IMF. Notwithstanding bravado stands of early principle, the hope for professionalism lay in the brilliant young Minister of Foreign Affairs, Petros Solomon, who attended the lectures with no privileges above those of his comrades. We became very good friends, and I would be invited to have dinner at his home, a modest rather non-ministerial abode, and we would get drunk on honey wine.

One night, Petros was very free with the honey wine. His wife, Aster Yohannes, was with us. At one stage, Petros began laughing. "You know, Stephen, my wife and I never argue, NEVER argue . . ." I politely asked why. "Because she can shoot straighter and faster than I can!" They were both laughing at this stage. And, indeed, it was true. Aster had been herself a crack liberation fighter. Very many of the Eritrean front line troops were female. There were frontline romances, and one was told to me of two fighters, male and female, who had been quietly falling in love but neither had dared say so to the other. One night, their patrol was ambushed by the Ethiopians. They were returning fire, but it seemed they were all doomed. The female fighter took a fatal wound. The male, beside her, suddenly realised that every dream was now shattered and, beside himself with love and despair, and frenzy, rose and single-handedly charged the Ethiopian lines, firing wildly as he did so. The Ethiopians were so amazed at this "lunatic" act that, momentarily, they ceased firing—before shooting him down. But the brief pause was just enough for his platoon to escape. One of the survivors, one of my students, told me this story. They were not going to be the world's best diplomats, no matter how hard I tried. I could never bring myself to criticise them harshly.

But I was asked to draft a preliminary sketch paper on demobilization of the liberation army. I spoke to some female fighters. "We don't want to demobilise." Why was that? "Here, we have achieved a recognised equality. We proved ourselves in combat. The Ethiopians were hard. They had Soviet officers. No one doubts our right to be equal. In civilian life, there is still the traditional inequality, and we would be subordinated." As it was, no demobilization occurred, for war was soon to be again a key option for the Eritreans.

They were good at war. One day Petros took me on the road that rolled down the steep hills atop which Asmara sat. We stopped when any trace of Asmara was out of sight and got out of the Landcruiser. "This is where I directed our artillery bombardment of the Soviet-held airport." I looked up, and then down. "Two questions: we came down a winding route; the airport would demand very precise targeting, and this is not a good location; secondly, how the hell did you get your artillery pieces up here in the first place?"

"The calculations as to trajectories, I did myself. How did we get the guns up here? That's a good question. The road is very steep and was barely passable then. I imitated General Giap at the Battle of Dien Bien Phu. The French thought they were impregnable. That Giap could never shell them. He couldn't haul artillery into the jungle mountains around the French base. Well, as you know, Giap took his guns apart and the Vietnamese carried them, piece by piece up the mountains, and reassembled them.[8] We did just that."

The bombardment was so effective that the Soviet advisers decided on withdrawal from Asmara. Petros became the city's "governor" until the Eritrean leadership arrived. I asked who else had influenced his military thinking.

"Clausewitz." I should add that Clausewitz is required reading at every single war college and officer training school on earth—the Prussian General who finally worked out how Napoleon was defeating his armies over and over again.[9] "Even with their Soviet officers and advisers, how we defeated the Ethiopians was to apply Clausewitz's dictum. Move faster than your enemy. Concentrate all your forces against his weakest point. Smash through faster than he can reorganise and reinforce." Which over three long (and unfinished) volumes (he died before he completed his writing), was pretty much Clausewitz in a nutshell.

But sometimes the Eritreans took a huge casualty toll. Petros was involved in one of the battles for Massawa. I was offered a day trip to the port city beside the Red Sea. Hooky declined to come. Even he needed a rest day. Driving the long, winding road down for some hours made me appreciate just how high Asmara is. I found Massawa in total ruins. Not a building was unscathed. I had not seen such devastation even in Uganda. But this, it turned out, was part of what the Eritreans were turning into atrocity tourism—both to make the point of how much they had overcome and how wicked the Stalinist regime had been, but also to see what stuff their foreign friends were made of. That "stuff" basically had not to flinch when taken to one of the Stalinist dictator, Mengistu's, execution sites. My minders opened the gates almost with a flourish. Behind a green roofing metal fence of sorts lay the remnants of several hundred Ethiopian officers and soldiers who had rebelled against the dictator. What was left of them was piled into ammunition crates. Skeletal remains dominated. Some bones retained gristle. It was grisly. I said I would want to file a report to the UK Foreign Office and calmly, taking my time, set about counting as best I could the bodies. 600. All I was thinking was that I hoped they died well, with bravery and dignity. It was the way of the dictator to smash all dignity out of the victim before despatch. This was something, as I found later, the Eritreans had learned from him.

Later, leaving my minders behind, I went for a walk on the long beach beside the Red Sea. No remnants of Egyptian chariots. Such musings filled my mind while looking back at the ruins of Massawa. A young boy fell into step with me and asked, in halting but understandable English, where I had come from. I said I had come from England. "Ah," he said, "we had terrible famine here nine years ago. We thought no one would help us. But my father says that there was an English singer then who did try to help us." That was all I needed to let the repressed anguish come through. Geldoff had been my near neighbour in Faversham, Kent. My evening runs to the Saxon Shoreway would take me past his house, a converted priory. So, I thought, sobbing beside the Sea of Moses, the old loudmouth really did come through.

Then the boy told me he came to Massawa every year to mourn his brother who had died in the battle for the city. The Eritreans had used suicide attacks against a dug-in Ethiopian garrison. When they triumphed, the Ethiopians replied—or rather their Soviet allies replied—by sending in wing after wing of MIG fighter bombers to drop phosphorus bombs on the Eritreans. It was this that destroyed the city as much as the battle itself. Those who survived felt they were invincible. But the boy's brother was not among them.

I made a number of visits to Asmara, slowly building the foreign service. On one visit I met up with Cirino Hiteng Akuffo, from South Sudan, then a PhD student at the University of Kent. Later, when South Sudan itself became independent, after a war of liberation that lasted a total of fifty years, he became a minister, and then became a political pawn in the terrible games that South Sudanese politics have become—imprisoned, exiled, recalled, never quite knowing where the winds of independence would blow him. But he had been a child soldier[10] and, being clearly very intelligent, had been taken by his commander to a Christian monastery to be educated. He came to Kent with a collection of check suits and a deep knowledge of wine—which they made at the monastery. On that visit, my mother was in hospital in New Zealand for colon cancer surgery. Effectively, he took me in hand and looked after me. This is the prose poem I wrote about his kindness to me in Eritrea. [11]

"Cirino"

Do you ever think of the time you shouldered a gun for Garang, those nights we walk in great cities? London? Vienna? I include Asmara, prize of the great campaign. You fantasised you could take Juba just like that? Ah, Cirino, and it is always wet: we, you and I, dodging puddles, cut on wine, discussing laughter and death, always death; our genealogies, like the litany of our scriptures, is always of the unseen cousin. Only you have seen more of him. The thunder flashes of battle. Between them there is only the straining for sound. You are deafened. You are trying to hear how close the tumbling cups of death are sloshing their liquefying business by your accepting but terrified ears. Not afraid. You're never afraid. You'd just like to know when. Even when the shellburst illuminates your face, it is merely pondering how small a word can make death as calm as . . . well, Vienna. When. If we knew, we could. . . . What? Die happy? Died prepared. Do it with more than a nanosecond's respect for a life you lived with integrity and resignation.

We discuss these things by hand signs, by gestures and eye flickers, one winter's night in Covent Garden. The others in the party are young in experience. They want the wine's glow under the brazier at my favourite streetside table. Summer or winter, I am seated there. You know where to find me. The fingers drum out the gunfire. The piazza is full of bodies. No one sees them. It is full of bodies. Where I sit, the table, is a convergent point. Battles come here and sit in the piazza. I think about the battles of the world, Cirino; about you trudging the Sudanese sands, an AK across your shoulder; how they decided there was learning in you and sent you to a monastery school and, by and by, cobbled scholarships later, you are in England. But I see gunfire in your eyes. I see the way you listen— peripheral hearing, a fox turning its ears for the sound bouncing off the cobblestones. The waist is thicker now; they taught you about wine in the monastery; but ready, in an instant, to swivel—body drop and flatten. The waist, Cirino, I saw from the waist first, then the ears and eyes, that you had been a fighter. No one else knows. My friends lead too polite and well-washed lives to need to know. You're just the refugee scholar in the check suits. Let them adopt

you like that. Let them not know how like wine on hands it all is,
this business.

And we couldn't talk either, that night riding back on a slow train
from Canterbury. You, freshly made a doctor of philosophy. I'd
watched you nervously waiting your turn in the cathedral cloisters,
the scarlet facings of your gown in the shadow. Then you emerged
briefly into the light mediated by the stained glass. Scarlet and
black—your colors, my colors since youth. You wave a red flag
against the night? Of course. It is the only thing to do against the
night. We tried to speak of this on the train. As if death washed over
our middle age, left its wrinkly scars, foreheads marked for a distant
but rapidly closing sniper. He takes those near you, one by one,
you're just listening as it happens, before the rifle turns (you hear
its swivel) toward you in a train, you in a piazza, me in a piazza.
The wine glass shatters. How glad it was the glass. We look up at
the same instant—a reverie, we come out of a reverie—the train
is crossing the Thames: there's the Albert Bridge to our left, with
all its lights; there's the high water; can't see the moon; the station
swallows us. When shall we see each other again?

And shall it be like that night in Asmara? Wet. You navigated me,
eyesight always better, around the filled potholes, walking back
from God knows where—where the common people eat and drink,
you said (and get drunk, I said later—and taking a cool two hours
to do it, stumbling (no, only I stumbled) until we gratefully encoun-
tered the paved sidewalks of the inner city. My mother is very ill, I
said, probably a cancer in the colon, and they should be operating
even as we walk. "These are the streets," you said, "down which
the victorious Eritrean army walked, amazed they had done it. The
Soviet officers and Ethiopian soldiers just evacuated to Addis. They
didn't try to hold. But they took all the university's library books
with them. In Mozambique, the departing settlers smashed all the
flushing toilets. Here, they knew in a more refined way how to slow
the birth of a new country. Stephen, how many books have you
dedicated to your mother? She is dreaming of them now. Even as
she lies there, the scalpels busy, that part that rises above keeps one
eye on the surgeons and the other in the great unlooted library of her
memory. She will live and grow better for you. She is remember-
ing you. A refugee child? She was well seated with us, all eating
with our fingers, in that humble café in the slums. Don't you know
I could see by the way you lifted your food, raised your wine glass,
that you were offering everything before it touched your lips? Me a
fighter? You're a priest. Before we part on this street corner—your
hotel's over there—let us pray for your mother that, for this time at

least, the love that comes from memory will flood away the impediments to the future."

Cirino, I said, once when I was in Asmara, my father was dying. I wrote about what I would do. I wrote it in this very city, how I would send a White Warrior to carry him easily to his new world. "Stephen, I think you will not do this again from Asmara. You will be with her, perhaps. Afterward, you will write about it. What will be the metaphor? The White Warrior again? Before you write, I shall put my arm around you, catch you in some city, somewhere. Be strong. I do not think your mother will die tonight. But, even though it is you who are the failed priest, it is I who have been around them more recently. Let me lead the prayer."

Many years after his graduation, I met Cirino again by chance. He was a minister now and South Sudan was reaching the agreed penultimate step in the negotiated transition to independence—an election. This was 2009, and I was an election observer. I conducted the observation both in Rumbek, where the war of liberation began—a backwoods town that looked like the wild west—and with a larger team in Juba, the capital. Muddy, pestilential, a city with almost no paved roads in a country the size of Germany with no paved roads at all. I trashed my vehicles on the route between Juba and Rumbek. There was meant to be peace now, but guns were everywhere. Landmines, with no maps as to where they were, lined the roadsides. I wouldn't let the female members of my small team urinate in the bushes. We opened both car doors and looked the other way as they relieved themselves on the road between. "Why can't I go into the bushes?" "Because you'll get your ass blown off." I shared my makeshift bathroom with a friendly colony of cockroaches. They're more intelligent than their legend suggests. We came to an arrangement whereby they got two minutes warning before I turned on the shower. They obligingly evacuated the shower-box and, two minutes after I turned off the contaminated water, they came back. I didn't kill any of them and gave their leaders names. The water was so contaminated that I cleaned my teeth with beer, and still got diarrhoea. But the road between Juba and Rumbek was a wilderness of magnificent large birds. Sometimes, on the banks of the numerous lakes we passed, some natural, some artificial as they had been created by excavations to pile more dirt on the rapidly eroding dirt roads, they would sit in a circle, as if in a parliament.[12] They would be the only parliaments that worked in a devastated country.

But there was one reasonable restaurant, open-air, beside the Nile. Italian food, foreign wines. It was the occasional treat. One night, restless, I got up from my table, leaving my team behind and walked a little along the edge of the Nile. I was still within sight of my table, and they saw me embrace a man who had emerged from the gloom of the night. It was Cirino. It was like meeting a long-lost brother. He bought champagne for my table, courtesy of the President's Office where he held his ministerial portfolio. We drank and smiled, and did not talk.

By then, I had written a suite of sonnets for my mother, Kwok Meil Wah, after whom I have now named a foundation. They remembered her time in hospital in a room looking out to Auckland's Waitemata Harbour and Rangitoto Island in the distance. And they look back to Cirino's prayer on the Asmara street corner, rain still falling, as I tried to project images of Eritrea and Ethiopia to her.

I

I am looking down on Ethiopia and it is wet
meaning, Meil Wah, people will live—and that
has a special resonance for you, the bright
hospital room escaped, encamped a tube-struck

stranger in your own home, and I, ah, I
am marching into the Addis transit lounge
with a one hundred-member white-clad choir,
sponsored by Coca Cola and waiting for their

connections. Thus are we all joined to our destinies and our
machines, mine an aerial Ethiop,
yours life-saving by the Auckland waters.

It is wet in Ethiopia, Meil Wah. One hour soon
the choir will sing, the dead will rise,
a flight of swallows will fan your eyes.

II

Now the lounge contains a hundred nationalities,
we are fighting for the ninety seats, and there are
turbans, young beauties, and of course the choir,
but here at last the captain is striding by

and he looks like the captain of any plane, and we
are instantly made one by our hope that
we shall be passengers again. When the captain
trained, Meil Wah, there was a dictator in Ethiopia.

I know his exile home. I know one hundred
transit lounges. I imagine here a pathway to the
sea, your sea, your home. I imagine the hills of Rome.

Fallen rulers, empires, stricken mothers are hallucinations
here. We cannot sleep, we do not fly, thirst-quenched
however, rain falls from the sky.

III
He was long-haired at birth, blacker than Chinese should
be, and sublimating an outrage only a Buddha's waters
of peace could drown, and not now, not yet on the
expectant, clamorous and poor plains and plateaux of

Africa. He's at it again, never learning, but Asmara's growing
And the avalanche of moral decline is, out of sight,
Unconsciously but methodically, structurally, massing its
Boulder strong might. On the green hills he is preaching

What is right and here, in Asmara, it is only temporarily
night and he is, despite his preoccupations, sending you
a son's loving greeting, Meil Wah, and not imagining too

much scars and tubing, but strength and healing. His
hair falls over his face and the shadows make bright
the lines of his age and he is, you would know, preparing to fight.

IV
The desert coffee's strong. Five to keep working this afternoon,
five hours sleepless tonight. You're awake too, Meil Wah,
twelve hours ahead or thereabouts, day for night and the
Pacific sun shines over your harbours.

As it did when you looked out your hospital room with
Rangitoto island in full view, and beyond it the clear waters
of the Hauraki Gulf, and beyond them the runaway continents,
the lands drip-fed where I almost live.

When you fell, trying to walk strongly towards Rangitoto,
images of beyond not quite in your head, and the tubes
ripped out, and waste and blood paletted slow-motion forth

it was the image of nausea and death that drove you, stumbling
still, towards the alarm. In these desert lands a banker comes
to one like you and says, heaven-voiced, rip out your tubes and
walk.

V
I do not begrudge them comforts. Look at the life I lead.
Why should not they reap rewards? But when I see the

Mercedes, the growing array of smaller luxuries, then I know
the slope itself will slide. I have one body, oh Eritrea,

telling me politely it will age. I wish to look on someone's
beauty when I am old. How shall I write my mother?
That I walked the streets tonight, that shadows are long,
the potholes are full of swallowed hearts.

Meil Wah, I am writing books of the fall. I see cherubim
Sword-arcing the gates. I pray it will rain on them all.
I pray no one has written the fates for an account of us

all. I pray you are healing. I pray you are laughing
at your narrow escapes, that you walk without stumbling in
your great halls, that you think of Asmara as I have projected it.

VI
Each night I expect to see him here, a loved companion
who died in the war, missing him like the brothers I never
had long, and he will tell me his story which I am
writing in a book to honour the idea of love and freedom

how he and she took up arms and fell in love at the
height of the battle, and how she died and he, knowing
the single dream of peace had gone, charge single-handedly
the enemy and, dying, saved his battalion and joined

the wife of a moment's flash of gunfire and unbridled
hope. My mother you too are the child of war and pursuits
and artillery bombardments, and you know precisely who

I am and how I can never requite the sacrifices
and, one day, I shall stand on some hill, the valleys
strange to me, and feel the need to charge forward.

VII
A grave day, no pun at all intended, but we inspected
how the dead lie, under combed sand if British, under
the shade of bougainvillea if Italian, many headstones
recalling no name known; in one, fragments of four

unknowns, and then we climbed to the highest point of
Keren and from there set out to find the memorials in
whose shadows the unnamed Eritrean dead lie.
They say 100,000 now, when I first came only

55,000, and it is the resonance of "only" that rocks
in my ears, and if there is freedom earned the hard
way, this is it. But not even this gives a licence

to rule forever, nor even to get used to the gaudy
trappings of rule. Meil Wah, it is raining in Eritrea.
I am to be laid under combed sand only.

Afterward, Cirino fell victim to the factional and militarised politics that tore the new nation of South Sudan apart. Fifty years of fighting meant that senior figures knew war as their major skill. Desperately poor infrastructure, such as the lack of paved roads throughout the country, and the lack of sanitation in the capital city, meant that development was in fact impossible, and quality of basic life tenuous. The international community poured in aid money but there was no way to spend it. Nothing worked, nothing could be delivered—so the money was appropriated; an oligarchic class developed; rival armies became better armed.

Untoward developments gathered pace in Eritrea too—albeit without conspicuous corruption. The president was largely ascetic and had a view of propriety matched only by his view of himself as rightly and deservedly autocratic. But war also was what he had known best and Eritrea never disarmed. Indeed, war footing was never retrenched. How this spilled into relations with Ethiopia, from which it had recently split but without full agreement on certain border demarcations, is taken up in the next chapter. But younger ministers, who had been young commanders, African equivalents of Napoleon's Young Marshalls—only President Isaias Afwerki was himself no Napoleon—were restless as autocracy set in. They had all been equal in battle. They had been brave and idealistic. They wanted, Petros among them, a new world. Afwerki began to give them a North Korea beside the Red Sea.

We worked in Eritrea, shuttling back and forth from the UK, training the foreign ministry from 1993 to 1997. We did the best we could, but I could sense the Eritrean desire to settle all disputes by force. They knew what victory tasted like. It is not necessarily militarization for its own sake. Victory is addictive.

What was it like on the Ethiopian side? After all, two armies had combined to overthrow the Stalinist dictatorship. Did the Ethiopian army, drawn largely from one province, Tigray, also have an unending desire to fight? The answer began to be delivered to me in 1998 when a consortium anchored in the University of Rotterdam approached me. They wanted to use my shuttle model in Ethiopia. They were going to train not just one ministry—but all of the cabinet, the high command, and all of the parliament; they were going to start from scratch and keep going until everyone had achieved a master's degree. Bring the entire governmental cadre from being liberation fighters to being adepts in a brave new technocratic world. Credentialise them, both so they would have something to aim for and something of which to be proud. Something to which they would commit. Would I be part of it? I said, "yes," and went to Addis Ababa over the 1998 to 1999 period. But war broke out between Eritrea and Ethiopia in 1998.

NOTES

1. H. W. van der Merwe, *Peacemaking in South Africa: A Life in Conflict Resolution*, Cape Town: Tafelberg, 2000, pp 138–150.

2. See Robert Scott Jaster and Shirley Kew Jaster, *South Africa's Other Whites: Voices for Change*, New York: Macmillan, 1993, p 98. This book also gives an appreciative account of van der Merwe's work and overall contribution to change.

3. My conclusions now are very much this was a direct South African action. This revises some benefit of the doubt I was prepared to accord in Stephen Chan, *Exporting Apartheid: Foreign Policies in Southern Africa, 1978–1988*, New York: St. Martin's, 1990, pp 52–54.

4. Published in the University of Calgary journal *Ariel: A Review of International English Literature*, 18:1, 1987, p 51.

5. https://www.tripadvisor.co.uk/Hotel_Review-g293789-d1574712-Reviews-Embasoira_Hamasien_Hotel-Asmara_Maekel_Region.html, 15 July 2020.

6. https://www.hollows.org.nz/freds-story, 14 July 2020.

7. https://natlib.govt.nz/records/23059190?search%5Bi%5D%5Bsubject%5D=Social+and+moral+questions&search%5Bi%5D%5Bsubject_authority_id%5D=-1488&search%5Bpath%5D=items, 14 July 2020.

8. Martin Windrow, *The Last Valley: Dien Bien Phu and the French Defeat in Vietnam*, London: Cassell, 2005.

9. Carl Von Clausewitz, *On War*, https://www.gutenberg.org/files/1946/1946-h/1946-h.htm, 15 July 2020.

10. For a deeply sympathetic treatment of South Sudanese child soldiers, the first study giving their own perspectives, see Christine Ryan, *Children of War: Child Soldiers as Victims and Participants in the Sudan Civil War*, London: I. B. Tauris, 2012.

11. Published earlier in Stephen Chan, *The White Door*, London: Nth position, 2012, pp 87–89.

12. See the chapters "Alice Who Almost Became the Witch President of Uganda" and "Veli Scena: Vijay and the Speech of the Birds" in Stephen Chan, *Joseph Kony and the Titans of Zagreb*, London: Nth Position, 2012, in which these birds become protagonists, agents, and nations in their own right, both in South Sudan and neighbouring Uganda.

Chapter 5

Facing the Tragedies

In 1998, Addis Ababa did not look like it does today. In just over two decades it has become a metropolis, its expansion being both a signal of huge modern development and the cause of great unrest by those whose lands were incorporated into the growth of concrete and glass. And although the government tried to build apartment blocks to rehouse displaced populations, memories and community cultures, especially those of non-Tigrayan peoples who viewed the government as representing an ethnic minority, could not be easily replaced by an ironically Soviet form of urban development. Row upon row of high-rise apartments were not a substitute for something communally intimate, settled, and old. Nor could it bring back the eagles who have been driven out of Addis. When I went there in 1998, it was a city of eagles.

It is not easy to describe this. Eagles as plentiful as sparrows in a London suburb. Eagles who danced in great patterns over Addis at sunset like vast formations of swallows. Eagles who sat on lampposts, danced in vertical spirals in the thin air—giving spectacular meaning to the line by Yeats, "Turning and turning in the widening gyre"—and looked like kings.

It was also a city with scorpions. Staying at the government's Ghion Hotel, superficially more palatial than the Embasoira, I was mistaken for the Japanese film director Nagisa Oshima. He had long hair then and, since this had already happened in Oslo, I decided it was meant as a compliment—despite my not looking at all like him. What Oshima would have done, or what film he would have made, if he had awoken one night to discover a mother scorpion bringing her children to feast on his body, is an interesting question. I didn't kill them, they clearly lived in that mattress, but did phone reception to bring a new mattress. Which, in the middle of the night, they did. Clearly this was not an unusual request.

The hotel then had extensive gardens, partly wild and undulating. You could wander and be out of sight of everyone. Not out of earshot of the busiest intersection in town, but isolated and peaceful enough for great eagles to sit in the tall trees above me as I tried to talk to them. The hotel cats would

71

wander out to sit with me. Shona sculpture from Zimbabwe featured in the grounds. Dictator Mengistu had been a close friend of Mugabe and, indeed, took exile in Zimbabwe. I once went out to view his mansion there, bolted and guarded; but did inspect the contents of his rubbish bins outside. Endless whiskey bottles. Losing power is clearly a sorrow best drowned.

But the intersection, a favourite on social media with traffic sped up, featured several convergent roads with nine lanes in each direction. There were no traffic lights and no traffic policemen or women. On the other side the poorer districts began. I discovered you had no choice but to walk out, cars slowed down, you could cross eighteen lanes either because of Ethiopian courtesy or because killing you would simply have delayed traffic further. I would walk in a straight line on the other side for thirty minutes. Straight so I could find my way back. I found a gym with a mud floor and signed up. No one blinked. I wasn't "normal," but, if not openness, the tolerance was impressive. The owner had been an Olympic champion. Not all such champions had become rich, but he would have counted the gym as a reasonable business. On the uneven floor, machines sometimes precariously balanced, some running machines acting as bridges across declines, people were working out exactly as elsewhere. Overweight women in leotards gamely trod the running machines. Men whose chests had seen firmer days were straining at their bench presses. All seemed normal in the era after liberation. As for my own workouts, I was simply trying not to be altitude sick. It was a fine line between going slowly and deliberately, and collapsing in a panting heap.

On my third morning in Addis I decided to have a good look at the line-up outside the hotel gates. Hawkers, beggars, but one or two offering walking tours of the city. I approached two of the younger men, aged I thought about seventeen, and said I didn't want to be guided around the normal sights. I wanted to see how ordinary people live. They said they could do that but, to get to some of the poorer areas, one of which I had already discovered, we would have to go past some of the sights anyway. "All on foot?" they asked. "All on foot." The ministers and parliamentarians I was teaching all had to work in the afternoon. They took two hours off each morning for my lectures which were about how to understand and face up to the international system with as little naivety and pre-formed doctrine possible. The afternoons could be spent walking the great city. "We have a tradition of kings here. They would never walk the same route twice. Never go back the way they came. Do not look for landmarks to guide your way home. You must rely on us." Which was a way of saying they would keep me safe. Gangs of unemployed youths would watch us walk and prepare an ambush for our walk back. Clearly the way of the kings was to live as long as possible.

They were Joseph and Daniel, good Biblical names. One saved the region from starvation, the other made friends with the lions sent to eat him. They were probably the only criteria I used in deciding to trust them. They had come in from the countryside and were technically students by virtue of having enrolled at the Alliance Francaise. They had learned no French at all, but the student card gave them exemption from conscription as war clouds loomed. They needed to feed their families in the countryside, so they lived together on the dirt floors of a derelict building which, on a succeeding trip, they took me to see. But many people were coming in from the countryside, including long lines of women following tall and narrow iron crosses—sometimes singing or chanting hymns that described, Joseph and Daniel told me, the end of days. Clearly the violence and upheaval of the war of liberation was not the last of their woes.

I put Joseph and Daniel on retainers, somewhat generous by local standards, and they were good to their word. One day we were in a suburb named Mexico. I never worked out why it was called that. When, years later, I went back to find it, it had become glass skyscrapers. Then it was like a giant *barrio*, a *favela* if one were to mix one's Hispanic languages. We found a huge *dojang*, Korean Tae Kwon Do training studio—again with mud floors, but with a female Ethiopian teacher. I introduced myself and said I practiced the Japanese and Chinese arts but had trained often with Tae Kwon Do teachers and, indeed, for a week with the North Korean team. She immediately said, "We had North Korean teachers here. Mengistu was a friend of both the Soviets and the North Koreans. When it was clear Addis would fall, the North Koreans evacuated. But they took with them all the black belt certificates they themselves had awarded us. I myself, as the sole senior teacher left, have no credentials." I said I would be back that night to watch her lead her class. I did take a taxi. I wasn't going to walk that distance twice in a day. She was good. But then she introduced me to her class of about forty students and asked if I might give them a demonstration. I was her guest, and it was impossible to refuse. So I performed a pattern from the White Crane system, saying that Ethiopia and the Far East shared the same bird. I became desperately breathless—my body still had not adapted fully to the altitude—but it was impossible to let it show. We parted on cordial terms, and I said I would help her. Back in London, I arranged for one of the national Tae Kwon Do bodies, solely on my recommendation, to issue a certificate of black belt rank to her. The mail worked, she received it, but I never found the *dojang* again and, as I said, Mexico is a suburb of skyscrapers now. Eagles and martial arts studios have been driven into the peri-urban areas, chased closely by the glumping modernizing metropolis.

One day, Joseph and Daniel walked me near the brand-new Sheraton Hotel. I was tired and said I would buy us all a drink. But the guards at the gate refused them entry. "You see, Mr Stephen, this is a place for the elite, and we look poor." I was infuriated. I said that, on my last day, after my lecture, we would come again. They were my size. I would give each of them one of my suits. I would Windsor-knot their neckties for them. We would have not just a drink, but lunch there. And we did. They kept the suits—although they would probably have sold them to pay the rent on their mud floor. But, for a day, they were kings.

But they were also very canny observers of psychology, intuiting where even casual remarks may have originated as I related some of my adventures to them. The long walks became almost highly subtle therapy sessions. They said they had been to the hidden temple of the Ark of the Covenant, and this had given them insight. They said they had heard sermons there in *ge'ez* the ancient language of the Coptic priests and which had been, like Latin in Europe, the written language of record. Christianity and writing had been theirs for as long as Christianity had been alive. God was with them. St George rode with them as they defeated the invading Italians. The Ark of the Covenant was in Ethiopia as the only place God knew that would keep it safe. "If it is not found, the end of days will pass over us."

"Addis: Walking on New Flowers"

I
You are Stephen,
St Stephen your church and your saint.
I shall call you Mr Stephen,
we shall walk the city
you will show restraint as I discern
your life, Mr Stephen, discuss with you
sin and your fate.

We have not long, Mr Stephen,
Some few days to wander,
never retracing our steps,
following the nuns with their crosses
their long iron crosses.
If it seems fast, we are running,
we are running with God, Mr Stephen.

Don't look alarmed, Mr Stephen,
the run with God softens our steps
the stones in the road are a carpet
we follow the nuns
who come in from the mountains
my mother among them
my mother went to join them
daily they pray

the world is redeemable
even if you, yourself, seem unredeemable.
Your distress is less
   because of their praying
   towards the day of all days.

You know that day, Mr Stephen.
You seek it and flee it in your planes.
You fly constantly.
Everywhere you find me
the lifelong guide you never avoid.
Leaving one city
landing, finding me
   I am Joseph
   My friend is Daniel—
Over and over again.

II
I see you watch the eagles fly, Mr Stephen,
I see you watch them wheel in the sky,
I watch you wanting to cry, Mr Stephen,
I see you wanting to sing.
The eagles wheel in the sunset
they roost in trees taller than turrets
at day's end they sit like satisfied kings.

III
You count the great birds
you said the great birds
   carry you above and between retributions.
What is this retribution, Mr Stephen?
And is there not a forest in the skies
where the Buddhist monk
   in his yellow robes
awaiting the birds on which you fly
can absolve this retribution?
What are you paying, Mr Stephen,
what terrible sin makes you comfortable
   only in the skies?

And I have seen the way you watch the eagles fly.
You watch as if you had no weight.
But you have no wings.
Did they amputate those when
they cast you out from the skies?

You asked to walk on flowers.
Flowers never lived in those bygone skies.

IV
The problem with you, Mr Stephen,
is that you walk on flowers
constantly
        walk
                on flowers
thinking you crush not a petal
thinking you are an unweighed ghost
the magus of the flowers
weightless, invisible as you please.

This is your legend, Mr Stephen,
the myth of your constant travels
the mantra you hum as you fly
silver grey unceilinged sky.

Do you walk on flowers in Heaven, Mr Stephen?
We gather red petals leached from the sky.

We smooth them out
post them on trees
guessing avenues where you'll walk,
delighting in flowers that speckle your hair
cushion your feet,
then we smooth them out again
sometimes arrange them like a heart
which you, head in the sky, might never see.

V
The cats speak only Amharic, Mr Stephen.
Don't think the language of planes can speak to them.
They sit among shrubs, topiarised like Shona sculpture
And, because the shrubs seem relics
        of when your heart
            first opened
you think the cats will sit at your side
while you recount them your days.

The cats speak only Amharic, Mr Stephen.
Their ancestors fawned on Magda,
she whom you call Sheba,
before she fell in love with Judah
        and with Solomon

all those generations
    I count two hundred
    and fifty
       to Menelik
And the cats have yet an imperial gaze.
They imagine catching the eagles of the sky,
connoisseurs of the feast
      mouths red
          as the eagles die.

The cats speak only Amharic, Mr Stephen.
They ignore you, when seated at your side.
They ignore your come-on line
      your
          best angelic phrase.

Have you read the Song of Solomon, Mr Stephen?
His overture to Magda,
she whom you call Sheba.
He called her a Shulamite,
she was dusky and lithe.
You thought once when you
      lay in her arms,
descended through daughters
      her arms,
you would smile wisely
      laugh wisely
       then die.

VI
There are parts of our south, Mr Stephen,
parts of our south
      where the flamingos fly.
You've never seen the flamingos fly,
blood pink against magenta skies.
You only think of eagles
      and the days they die.
Eagles are not the only
       rulers
           of the sky.

By the Covenant, Mr Stephen,
by the Ark of the Covenant
      where the priest veils his head
      and the fire melts his veil

and his eyes greet each day
                    monochrome
           burnt black and white
           like his nights,
by the Ark, Mr Stephen,
flamingos

(by the angels that bow
by the angels that vow
to defend the Covenant)

flamingos wheel
                    deal out the stars
                              sigh out the sigh
of angels who circle the skies.

****

And if flamingos play angels
What then are eagles?
Oh, Mr Stephen, on whose side did you war
in the great war of the skies?

VII
So, what memory's the memory of the strife in the skies?
I'll tell you five truths if you abandon your lies.

The flamingos carried the gift of Michaelangelo.
Priests carry a magic Bible on a belt by the heart.
To speak Ge'ez is to make each word an amulet.
When we were fighters, we stole into Addis
                    knowing all the back ways.

You know a woman, the daughter of Magda,
you lay in her arms in a dream
                    you dreamt seven old years ago
her name just means Early, she comes to you early
you know when you know her
it's a name of old endings.

Do you want a beginning?

In the high altitude you burn your lungs
and turn to a page in Ge'ez that says
the last days are upon us.

You must move early or never
early or never.
Look at the eagles.
When storms rage their eyes turn to silver.

Ethiopia has a huge heritage: the only country in Africa not to have been colonized; the oldest Christian liturgy in the world; a written priestly language into which the Bible was translated; a claim on being the location from which the Queen of Sheba came (in the Ethiopian tradition she was called Magda, and went to test her own wisdom against Solomon's); a long line of emperors that, legendarily at least, traced its genealogy back, name by name, to King David; and the defeat of the Italian army in modern warfare at the Battle of Adwa in 1896, when both sides fielded modern rifles and artillery—which the Ethiopians nevertheless reinforced with traditional armoured cavalry. In all the street markets of Addis Ababa, and this was very true of the old Somali Town, you could buy real or meticulously faked Bibles on goatskin written in *ge'ez* and paintings of Magda setting forth to dispute with Solomon, and the battlelines of Adwa.

In this setting, and especially after victory against a Soviet-supported dictator, one might have expected overmuch pride for a concentrated and condensed programme of studies that, no matter what its developmental purposes, still had to satisfy the standards required of the University of Rotterdam. The prime minister himself, however, led the way. It was only much afterward I discovered he had been one of my students. When I was finally told, I protested that his name, Meles Zenawi, featured in none of my records. "He took a false name, Stephen, so he would not receive any special privileges from you. He sat in your classes and the other classes alongside all the other students, sat the same exams, and wrote his own essays." He became renowned as a technocratic leader who gained the respect of the wider world—even though he and his government were not without controversy. I was simply blessing my socks that no one wanted to shoot any delegation from the IMF.

But war broke out in 1998 over border mapping disputes. I was clearly distraught. I pleaded with both sides not to fight. Between 70,000 and 100,000 were to die until the war ended in 2018. The commanding General of the Ethiopian side, on the eve of going to the front, invited me to dinner. It was done with care. A Chinese restaurant on the edge of the city, Ethiopian wine. Completely reasonable food—unlike what I had found in the only Chinese restaurant in Asmara. Toward the end of dinner, he sent the minders outside. "I know you are upset about this. I know Petros Solomon is your good friend. What can I tell you about how I also feel? Petros is my cousin."

They were to face each other again but may not have done. For Petros, having been demoted from foreign minister to fisheries minister, was arrested in Eritrea in 2001, for objecting to the need for war, and co-signing a public letter asking for the democracy for which he and the other signatories had fought. Afwerki, by now in full North Korean mode, had them all arrested and thrown into prison. His wife, Aster Yohannes, was in New York and telephoned me distraught and saying she was going to return to plead for her husband. I urged her not to do it, to let me do what I could. I rang the Foreign and Commonwealth Office. I was advised gently but firmly: "Stephen, do nothing. The European representative in Asmara just tried to protest and was immediately expelled. If you try something it will only make matters worse for him." Aster was arrested at the airport when she landed. Rumours are varied. Aster, it is said, died of illness in prison. Some say Petros still lives in terrible prison conditions. My information is that one day he was put in a cage, taken to the desert, left without water and, some hours later when he was crying from thirst, shot like a dog.

In trying to live the international, this was the greatest disappointment of my entire effort. I never went to Eritrea again. In the full worldly range of emotions, I realised I would personally shoot Isaias Afwerki.

Chapter 6

Facing Down History

Being Chinese involved a performance of great ambivalence. Looking Japanese, they always said, but exuding the serenity of the stereotype from antiquity while looking resolutely—like a socialist realist poster—toward the future. And without a racism toward Japanese, Koreans, Russians, Americans, the British, and Africans. It is important to offer a differentiation here born of popular prejudices that had developed within a vast, advanced, but highly isolated society. Japanese, both because of recent antagonisms, war, and a protracted invasion of China; and an antique bias which maintained that the race was descended from an exiled Chinese Princess and an island of apes. Koreans, because they ate too much garlic and were hermits on a backward peninsula. Russians, because they had red hair including body hair, were therefore part ape, ugly and, above all, related to demons who also had red hair. Americans, because they were ignorant and vulgar, boastful, lacking manners and finesse. The British because they were perfidious, hypocritical, and conquered too many people. Africans because—and this deserved no elaboration, being obvious—they were black devils, therefore evil and, above all, backward, more profoundly like apes than even the Japanese and Russians, and visibly unclean.[1] This cocktail of prejudices was inflected into all discussion by my grandparents. And Maoris were, of course, related to Africans in terms of their essential characteristics, especially that they were unclean—a view shared, although publicly disowned, by very many *pakeha* or white New Zealanders. And, even if these views could not be substantiated, what was obvious was that the Chinese were in any case superior to all of them, and that prejudices were simply a casual by-product of this obvious superiority.

All the same, and I only learned this after my father's death—it happened when I was very young—there was a Chinese market gardener in Mangere, then the outskirts of Auckland, New Zealand, who had married a Maori woman. He was a market gardener, just as my father was a greengrocer, because residual discriminatory law meant that Chinese could only occupy and exercise certain vocations. We didn't all volunteer to be laundrymen. So, we, like the Maoris, faced discrimination. Even so, when the market gardener died, the family heads of the Chinese community convened to discuss whether to attend his funeral. For his Maori wife and Maori in-laws would be there. My father, one of the youngest present, stood up and said: "You are without honour. I, for one, will certainly attend the funeral. He was one of us and, by marriage, they also are one with us." The elders were shamed, and all went to the funeral. When, decades later, I learned this, posthumous pride welled in me like a fountain.

Simultaneously, the last days of Sun Yat Sen's ill-fated Republic in the 1930s, even as it faced the Japanese invasions—the Japanese, with more modern weapons and better general-ship sweeping Chinese armies before them[2]—were ones of admiration for the United States in particular. John Woo's film, *The Crossing*, and Bertolucci's film, *The Last Emperor*, portray how, especially in cities like Shanghai, Hollywood had its impact in terms of fashion, affectations of behaviour, music, and ballroom dancing. The United States was named *Meiguo*, "The Beautiful Country," and Britain was called, *Yinguo*, "The Brave Country." Inescapable admiration was mixed with inescapable contempt—the contempt in part being overcompensation for having fallen so far behind technological prowess and international capacity. As for Japan, it was historically called *Wakoku* in the Tang Dynasty, the dynasty that epitomized the height of Chinese cultivation: "The Land of Inferior Dwarves." In a way, the ruthlessness of the Japanese toward China in the twentieth century owed to their own sense of having something to prove. You reap what you sow, and it was the determination of the Communist regime of Mao, after a most uncertain start, to prove to the world both that it was again on the path to superiority, but that, officially at least, it would look down on nobody. And this included Africa. Even so, China was clearly destined to be again the Middle Kingdom. I have always viewed this to be a not fully accurate translation. It is the Central Kingdom. The Centre of the World. Under Heaven but the Central Pillar that Supports Heaven. Meaning that it is Key to the Universe. In a way, my people—for I cannot escape being viewed as a Chinese person, no matter what my internal ambivalence—are the most conceited people on earth.

Even so, the effort in official terms to view Africa as a younger brother—since, if it was not equal it could be made so by elder brotherly care and assistance—was profound. This was caused by isolation in the Cold War and China's search for allies. This search began to prioritise what was called the "third world" in the 1950s, not even half a dozen years after Mao won victory. In 1955, at a summit of Afro-Asian nations in Bandung, Indonesia—what was the forerunner of the Non-Aligned Movement, Chinese premier Zhou Enlai made a startling intervention. He outlined a Chinese commitment to assist the "third world," and he also guaranteed non-interference in domestic affairs, that is, he committed China to the principle of sovereign independence. This meant there would be no public Chinese criticism of even outrageous behaviour by an independent state. This also meant of course that China expected no criticism of its own internal policies. Even so, it was a statement of political non-conditionality. Your internal politics were your own business, but China would still help. It was, in many respects, one of the great speeches of the post-war twentieth century.[3]

China would help, would not interfere—but could still lead. This was the essence of the Three World Theory put forward by Chairman Mao in 1973, its announcement carefully timed to suggest that a recent visit by Zambian president Kenneth Kaunda had put the key finishing touches to a doctrine with which the African "philosopher-king" agreed. It divided the world into three poles: a first world of combined U.S. and Soviet imperialism; a second world of the undecideds like Central Europe; and a third world of the newly emancipated developing nations, of which China was one, but which would implicitly cluster around China to oppose the first world and seek to win over the second. It was a doctrine of solidarity to be sure, but also one of centrality in the emerging world, with an eventual claim to centrality overall as the first world was faced down by combined moral censure.[4] Solidarity, centrality, and certainly naivety—as China soon found it was easier said than done to face down superpowers, and also refrain from acting like one. It found it easiest to refrain from acting at least, and at first, like a colonial power in Africa.

There has never been a static Chinese policy toward Africa. It has been developing since Zhou Enlai's Bandung statement in 1955, setting the tone for China's engagement with Africa as the continent began attaining independence a few years later. It has gone from quite pure-minded but large-scale infrastructural projects—seeking chiefly diplomatic support in return during the Cold War years—then certainly entered a competitive phase with the Soviet Union in supporting rival liberation movements. Its chief success was supporting Robert Mugabe's forces in what is now Zimbabwe. But there were conspicuous gaps in China's continental coverage, for example, South Africa and Nigeria bear little conspicuous or dominant Chinese imprint.

China continued to differentiate itself from the West in terms of making available liquidity flows, contrasting its methodology from that of the Washington consensus in the lack of conditionality. But, from the 1990s, it became clear that China sought long-term access to mineral and petroleum resources, even if those were a long way upstream. For those, China was prepared to play a long game. For that reason, it continued its liquidity flows, both by way of loan finance and direct investment. Most of this was on a state-to-state basis.

The historical lack of conditionality has meant that African governments were slow to react to two things: the upsurge of private Chinese investment and direct Chinese citizen penetration of the continent and its economies over the last fifteen to twenty years; and the transition from a state-lending model to one using Chinese banks.

With the use of banks, normal, even if generous, financial conditionality began to apply. Collateral by way of national assets was sought. It is the claims against collateral, coupled with citizen disquiet over the behaviour of private Chinese nationals in their countries, that has engendered what may be called the beginning of a new era of African resentful dependency. With exceptions, for example, Angola and Ethiopia, African negotiating capacity with China remains limited—the sums Beijing is still prepared to make available remain too large to resist or reject.

Beijing is also demanding greater transparency in the use of funds it gives. It would not rescue Mugabe or Mnangagwa's government with standby budgetary support because it felt it would be throwing good money after bad. Curiously, it was the Chinese demand for greater financial transparency in Angola that allowed the current government to pursue the members of the predecessor government, particularly the Dos Santos family, for corruption. Corruption was now more readily traceable.

So there is a mixed picture here, and a complex one—but an era of difficulty is indeed now beginning.

Even so, the scale of Chinese economic penetration is now something the West, unless it acts as a united entity—which it doesn't, and can't, as so many national interests are involved—cannot match.

The several stages of Chinese presence and strategy in Africa can be expressed in a pointed timeline:

1. Genuine help without preconditions, although clearly seeking political good will and diplomatic support; largely centred on infrastructural projects.
2. A conscious move toward infrastructural projects with political purposes (e.g., the Tazara Railway).
3. The formation of a doctrine of solidarity in the "Three World Theory," with Chinese leadership of the righteous pole of power. Concurrently, there was:
4. A taking of sides in political struggles, notably liberation struggles, choosing wrongly as in Angola, but correctly as in Zimbabwe, but notably absent to all intents and purposes in South Africa, so this was patchy.
5. A movement toward financial support, again in contradistinction to the manner of support provided by the West, but with a clear view to long

term benefits of a material nature (e.g., in resource expropriation); this is state-to-state in the first instance.

6. An early model by which partnerships were entered with local partners (e.g., parastatals), even if this meant Chinese (re)construction of derelict parastatals.

7. The beginnings of visibly increased private Chinese investment and businessmen operating on location in African countries.

8. A variation of this model into loan finance, foreign direct investment using Chinese firms of a commercial nature, and a movement away from state-originated financial support to that from Chinese banks.

9. A bifurcated model in which negotiations emerge between "equal partners" or partners at least with equal negotiating capacity, and benefits that can be exchanged of some equal value (e.g., the cases of Angola and Ethiopia), but in which dominant Chinese "partnership" persists with weaker states.

10. Commercial leverage in a more clearly commercialized relationship where collateral is called in, resulting in Chinese control in varying ways of state apparatus in other countries, (e.g., airports, that is, the beginnings of conditionality)—not political, but certainly at this stage financial. But the volume of investment is such, in a confused picture of public and private, that the entire process is hard to resist.

The early stages were, in Chinese thought, an extension of Confucian piety. Notwithstanding benefit to China, even if only at first by way of diplomatic support as the West sought to isolate it, the idea or justification was that Chinese policy expressed *Guanxi*, reciprocity, but within a vertical hierarchy that was not meant to be exploitative; it was meant to confer benefit; but for benefits extended downward, respect was owed upward. It is the exact opposite of the horizontal model of Western equality and democracy.[5]

In this model, huge outreach was accorded Africa. But social conservatism and historical prejudice remained an inescapable factor. It was frowned upon to marry a non-Chinese, and marrying an African would be beyond most social pales. Despite official discourse, that remained a boundary that was almost absolute. The most distinguished exception was the rise of Gabon's Jean Ping, product of a Chinese immigrant father and an African mother, who became one of Africa's most distinguished diplomats.[6] But he was an exception. And it is not to say there was not solidarity from early generations of Chinese migrants to the African cause.[7] In 1955, in Kliptown, Soweto, site of the 1955 Congress of the People, which began the fightback against Apartheid with the Freedom Charter, the 3,000 delegates—before they were violently dispersed by the police—were fed by a Jewish butcher and a Chinese greengrocer.[8] Early kung fu movies depicting black American fighters enacting Chinese martial arts—Jim Kelly, Ron Van Clief—suggested a sort of solidarity among anti-heroes at least.

It was with ambivalence of various sorts that I made my first visit to China in 2007. I had been invited much earlier to accept prestigious visiting appointments but had refused until every single member of the Politburo that had authorized the killings at Tiananmen Square in 1989 had either died or was near death. In 2007, this was the case. I had not sought to become involved in the emerging issues of Chinese–African relations. The person to blame was Dan Large, then an active PhD student at SOAS and now a faculty member of the Central European University. He was convening a conference in Cambridge with Ricardo Soares de Oliveira in 2006 and stormed into my office demanding that I agreed to be a speaker. "After all, you're Chinese and you're an Africanist," he said. "If you don't act as a bridge, who will?" I gave a paper that warned those already eyeing a prospective bandwagon that there were key traps for the unwary.[9] People have nonetheless almost rushed to fall into them ever since.

There followed an invitation from the Brenthurst Foundation, led by Greg Mills and endowed by the Oppenheimer family, but establishing itself as a key actor in Track 2 diplomacy. It was, in fact, not so much Track 2 as Track 1.5, and I myself described it as Track 1.25.[10] This was because its methodology of intervention in international affairs was to convene groups of high-level personnel, some serving ministers but, for the most part, retired ministers, senior officials, senior military officers (including generals), and even prime ministers and presidents. All people certain to have their telephone calls returned. To these would be added a smattering of engaged scholars with worldly experience. There was therefore no naivety in these groups, although there certainly was the kind of late-life idealism of those who had reflected on their tenures of power and, even now, wanted to do better. The groups would be convened for three sessions of deliberations, with the aim of producing comprehensive sets of principle which could guide today's political figures and states-people. The attraction was that these sessions would be convened in different parts of the world. The Tsvalu private game reserve of the Oppenheimer family was one such venue, the Konrad Adenauer Villa beside Lake Como another. This invitation to a set of sessions to establish principles governing trade between Africa, on the one hand, and China and the United States, on the other, featured Tsvalu, Washington, DC, and Beijing. I was to be part of the African delegation featuring the deputy chair of the African Union, Patrick Mazimhaka (number 2 to Jean Ping), former Angolan prime minister Lopo Do Nascimento, and South African cabinet minister Sydney Mufamadi—among others. The U.S. delegation featured former assistant secretary of state Chester Crocker—who had negotiated the South African withdrawal from Angola and Namibia[11]—several figures from the State Department, and such ambassadors to the UN as Andrew Young. At first glance, the Chinese delegation seemed lacklustre, but they were advisers to members of the Politburo. Basically, the amount of experience concentrated around the conference table was immense. What the Chinese did lack, however, was good research. Their in-depth knowledge of African politics was appallingly rudimentary, based only on government-to-government contacts—so no sense of opposition views or strength—and scholarly work which was always careful to toe the party line. It has improved a lot since then, but that was a true shock. The Chinese were convinced they were doing good toward Africans. If this was a benevolent but condescending Confucianism, the U.S. position was also a form of haughtiness. Everything, whether expressed by a member of a previous Democrat or Republican administration, began with American interests—to which, almost as a justification, were attached American values expressed as an accomplished freedom and democracy that others had unfortunately yet to achieve.

The bemusement of the African delegation was a sight to behold. Knowing Africa had to trade with both and hoping for some kind of competition that Africa could leverage, it was clear to the highest level delegation of the three that the continent was not being taken with the fullest seriousness.

The final set of agreed principles was worthy, and the entire exercise had laid down some key markers.[12] It is remembered as important and, in a way, it was. But it was also a display of diplomacy—whether Track 1, Track 2, or in between—as a form of pageantry; the great and the good discussing something worthy; and, in great halls, especially in Beijing, with the obligatory square flower box surrounded by the tables of each delegation, with the chair and his secretariat's table at the top, talking about benefit to the poor. The Africans and Americans faced one another, the Chinese faced their own chair.

Beijing was not without amusement. The Chinese privately approached me to ask why I was sitting with the Africans. "After all, Professor Chan, if you really wanted to help Africa you should surely be sitting with us." Sydney Mufamadi and I had much fun, both of us having transited on different flights through Moscow, and both of us having had our luggage mislaid at Moscow. I arrived before Sydney and immediately found a tailor at the shopping mall opposite my hotel and re-equipped myself for the opening ceremony on the following day. When Sydney arrived, I took him to the same tailor—who had never measured a black man before. Sydney took his time, in front of a startled clientele deliberately fingering every gaudy necktie in the entire shop.

And I discovered I had much in common with Chester Crocker, many of whose policies toward Africa I had opposed when he was in the Reagan administration. On the day off in Beijing, many delegates took advantage of an offer to visit the Great Wall. That day there was going to be an icy wind there, so "Chet" and I decided instead to visit the Temple of Heavenly

Peace. I wanted very much to see this temple for its architecture, minutely detailed in of all things a Hong Kong sword and sorcery comic book series called "Heaven and Earth," *Tien Ha*, the Chinese term for the universe which depicted its vertical nature, earth under heaven. The Red Warrior, poisoned by dragon's venom and turned wicked, is challenged by his former martial arts classmate and the battle takes place, frame by frame, aspect of architecture by aspect of architecture, over several pages against the backdrop of the Temple of Heavenly Peace.

It was just as depicted in *Tien Ha*, beautiful and indeed funnelling upward toward peace. I discovered then what a "liberal Republican" was like and understood from that and several subsequent experiences in Washington, DC, how such people are often even more affronted by Donald Trump than Democrats. For all the implicit foundation of U.S. "values" on display in Beijing, an administration without any values at all is a disaster. It also makes, for the Chinese and others, the predictability of American policies impossible. What interests? What values? Where is the U.S. long game?

As for the long game of China, if that was also based on an imperfect understanding of the world, especially Africa, then it was a situation ripe for all the old Chinese chauvinisms to settle into an expansion into a "dark continent." I wrote two essays in literary style on plane rides for a subsequent visit—thankfully without any further luggage delays—and in the days before the internet made escape impossible. Here is the first:

It is always the same. As soon as I reach airside I feel safe. I enter a place where no one can ask me to be of service to them. It is a place of asylum and immunities rain upon me. Once on the aircraft, the immunities are vouchsafe. They become invulnerabilities. They become reasons for my constant travel. They become rationales. The hours in the air become those brief days between incarnations promised the Tibetan believer, when the gods come to reiterate the meaning of life, or lives, and promise futilities in the aeons to come. But, for now, the futilities recede and stretch into distances that are no longer part of the self. The undistracted self sees the Ural Mountains below, sees the naked lower back of the curled woman reclining in the next seat, turned to the window and the sunset with the Russian rivers untold metres below. One day I shall plunge from an aircraft such as is toward those rivers, feel the cold burn my body, feel the wind tear back my face, feel my eyes water and cloud and my hair blown back like a concrete helmet flying upward as I fly down. Feel death as a cascading upward toward me, and fight to retain consciousness to face it, to greet it, to enter that brief time between one life and its one death. Now the sunset is gone. A steel grey is all I see. I also shall soon sleep an hour to awake over China— and, you know, I also am Chinese and I am flying to a land of immensities that my parents once fled, and I am flying to the northern capitol that they never saw, and I am telling my hosts on arrival that I am the son of a great yearning to be rid of China while being drawn to it. And I am the child of the morning star who would damn Beijing if I could, bomb its concrete boulevards and wave a sword of wonder across its sleepy faces.

But that will not do as I line up in the meticulous passport queue, hand over my three forms, search on the carousel for my luggage—indescribable except black like any other—and feel demand and service call me back as the black car comes ever closer to the hotel where, already, far too many people know I will stay. And I will put on a black suit and sit at a very long meeting—the man who didn't fall from the aircraft, the man who didn't meet the Tibetan gods, the man who had a brief asylum but who was only a passenger. The man who missed seven hours of yesterday but who has put in eye drops so that no one knows he has skipped across time zones and his body is asleep while his face and eyes act out the livelihood they have rehearsed so often.

The man gets away with it. And, in getting away with it, I re-enter that world of apartness. I didn't need the rest you needed. I didn't need to recover. I came at you, and it was you who stepped back.

Beijing is flat. Traffic thunders through it. Policemen with white gloves direct the cars, look at my jay-walking habits with disapproval, but I am clearly lost and being crushed by a truck at one intersection will be the same as being crushed at any other. If I don't die from their exhaust fumes first. But my hosts don't know where I am either. The thought heartens me until I rediscover my landmark. I re-set my jaw. I shall be only five minutes late.

Will there be time to see the Temple of Heaven again? There was a Hong Kong comic which, every week for years, was centred on that temple. Heaven and Earth was the comic's name—meaning the Universe, meaning heaven and everything under Heaven. Long-haired heroes would duel in the skies to claim ownership of magic swords. Flying meant they never tripped over their long robes and hems and, from week to week, their world was not dishevelled, and a sword lost one week could be reclaimed amidst much clamour and ardour the next. The artist captured the Temple as if he were an architect. But when I last saw it the sky was blue and there were no vapour trails overhead. Old men played Tai Chi and choirs practised in the surrounding parks. There were picnics and tourists and recitals on old instruments. Souvenir shops. You could buy a tiny emperor's costume for a three-year old nephew, a flag of China, a miniature dragon.

I change into a dark blue suit for the next meeting. I surmount my name badge with a tiny sticker of the Temple. Inside the conference chamber there is a flower bed between my delegation and the Chinese. They think I look Japanese anyway, so there is no incongruity that I sit with the foreigners. But I exude foreign-ness. The hair, the way I walk, the way I hold my body—but I think they are amazed I seem to love the Africans I advise more than I love them. There is, after all, an ancestry which should let them claim me, foreign-ness and all, before and beyond anyone else. But there is to be a balancing in the world: the Chinese certainly against the Americans; but the Africans on equal footing to them both. Not as a continent that auctions itself and its minerals to bidders from

East and West. Pay attention to us, is the African claim. Take us seriously. Does not everybody have the right to fly in the heavens with a magic sword? Does not everybody have the right to even the briefest immunities? To find a place at the intersection of historical epochs in which to rest from being plundered and to feel safe from being enslaved.

When you fly into Beijing, the final hour is over mountains. This is where the Beijing wind comes from, where it swirls and gathers before spiralling down to the flat city. This is where you recheck the spelling and visa numbers on your three forms. This is where you begin to be bureaucratised back into existence. You are about to land. But no one in this incarnation knows anything about your last. You do not carry the harassment that drove you into Heathrow. You emerge in Beijing, and they see you anew. They greet you as a stranger. Among them they remark on your strangeness. You drive into the city, breathing deeply, brows furrowed. With exhilaration swear at the suburbs sprawling past.

The trip referred to was arranged by Paul Moorcraft, an adventuring scholar and former military instructor who offers creative interventions to the world's problems. In this case, he brought to Beijing, at the invitation of the Ministry of Foreign Affairs and Chinese Academy of Social Sciences, a group of actors in the Darfur conflict. At that time, Beijing was much accused, particularly in the United States, of siding with Sudanese president Bashir, and thus riding a sort of shotgun over Khartoum's depredations in the province. The Chinese had played no active role in Darfur and wanted a way to maintain links with Khartoum and get itself off the Darfur hook. Sudan had been the fourth African country to offer China diplomatic recognition in the days when the United States sought to isolate China as an international pariah. Obligation now meant that Beijing could not disown Khartoum. But Chinese research and intelligence on the situation was characteristically weak. Thus, there was willingness to hear out Moorcraft's delegation. He would later mount one of the official electoral observations in Sudan in 2009, in which I participated, as the countdown to South Sudanese independence began. On this visit to Beijing, in 2007, I was there in part because of my conversation with Nigerian General Agwai, commander of the African Union and United Nations peacekeepers in Darfur, and because several of my martial arts students were part of the ZamBat (Zambian Battalion) in the thick of the peacekeeping. I had an appreciation of the situation from top and bottom. From the bottom, the peacekeepers were sitting ducks, deployed, but without mobility against highly mobile militarised factions. Roads and rail were scarce facilities in a province that was larger than Germany. From the top, command was an exercise without options.

I asked General Agwai, "What do you need?"

"Helicopters."

"How many do you have?"

"Two."

So he was trying to hold down the peace with his soldiers as sitting ducks, without any aerial reconnaissance capacity, and with no aerial attack capacity.

"What do you use the two helicopters for?"

"To fly to the funerals of my men."

I had already gone to the Ministry of Defence in Whitehall and raised the issue of helicopters. "We have absolutely none to spare," was the reply. So, at the height of Chinese proclamations in the conference that they were doing all they could, I said "What you could do is send 100 helicopters." There was consternation. I was asked to justify everything I had said. However, I had prepared a deployment grid and a logistics grid and a personnel list—all in the round, but it was enough for a strange invitation to come to dine that night at the private restaurant of the Chinese Liberation Army's high command. But, when I arrived, the restaurant was empty apart from the waiters, my interpreter, and myself. As we began dinner, I said to my interpreter that I thought I was meant to be explaining myself to persons unknown at this restaurant. "Start speaking, Stephen. They're listening." So it was I delivered my helicopters plan to the hidden microphones. China didn't send helicopters, but immediately announced an increase in its number of peacekeeping soldiers. There then began a series of highest-level visits to Khartoum, involving both the Chinese prime minister and even the president to pour polite but firm pressure on President Bashir to reduce his militarised profile in Darfur. Which he slowly did. Whether the visit of the Moorcraft delegation had anything to do with it is unclear. Moorcraft speculates about this in his own account.[13] But the flight back demanded some exorcism of the "hidden ways" of Chinese diplomacy, and I wrote about the allegory of the legendary Monkey story from the sixteenth century.

There are three versions of the Monkey King on Chinese television. And a fourth rather bad animation on the aircraft channels. None of them is good, but one of them has actors who believe their subjects. They are all about Monkey and his two companions—of whom one is a humanized pig—escorting a pious and naïve monk across the Himalayas to India to discover the Buddhist scriptures. He must battle legions of demons all the way, and thus face a different demon king every day on the never-ending television renditions of the epic journey.

But Monkey is doing this as recompense. It is his purgatory. A thousand years ago—maybe ten thousand years ago—he rebelled against Heaven. And failed of course. He was first pinioned under a mountain for a thousand—or ten thousand—years, then offered the chance of forgiveness but only if he played a leading part in bringing the scriptures back to China and thus converting a vast nation. Well, not really converting the nation. People, and monks, were Buddhists by intuition. They needed only schooling—rigor, guidance, and prohibitions. Monkey established the forbear of the Party and was inducted into Heaven for his pains—and probably those of the Chinese people today. Watching only one of the Monkeys on television, and his running around on clouds, one hoped that today at least a demon king might finally teach the Simian rascal a lesson. Like smash his simpering hairy face in. Crush his smug temples. Ram his golden quarterstaff up his ass until it shot out of his gaping mouth.

For two days, Beijing has been cloaked by desert dust, exhaust fumes, and a pharmaceutical haze. The streets are scrubbed, and trees and flowers have been planted and manicured everywhere—but it's a truly filthy city in which the Olympic athletes will have to run. You can't drink the water, and you can't breathe the air. You swelter in the summer heat and it's not dry heat; the humidity is composed of the chemical wash that bathes the skin like an irradiated glow. And when will the Party bosses, gliding by in their air-conditioned black Lincolns, windows smoked and with privileged number plates, do something about it?[14] It is the vengeance of the demon kings, as day succeeds day, and the visitor chokes to death and the resident thinks foulness is normal.

And, if you're a rich resident, the escape is in glamorous nightclubs and restaurants, architect-designed and with no expense spared (since it will be recouped from your bill). If you're less rich but a certain form of scholar—one whose research echoes and flatters the Party line—your life is a succession of conferences with banquets to impress the foreign delegates, and constant travel to their countries where the conference is reciprocated, and you write many conference papers that are published as monuments to Partyism, and declare yourself Great Sage just like Monkey, add gloss to scripture and think in your prescribed travels you are learning about the world. And, if you are poor and bring out your cot to sleep on the footpaths at nights—your room airless and without air-conditioning—you will soon be able to see the world's athletes pounding the marathon streets and suffering in a way for which all that training in high mountains and thin oxygen never prepared them. Oh, and there'll be thin oxygen alright. And much by way of cocktail besides. But I don't think the Politburo has run many marathons lately. No one on the Central Committee would last a Long March today. All is well with what they see of their ordered world as they drive sealed and smoothly by.

When Monkey brought back the scriptures, he was made a member of the Central Committee of Celestial Buddhas. He was called Victorious in Strife. He was issued his limousine and asked to stop his cloud-soaring. Promoted and grounded he sold the rights to his image to competing television channels and retired to live off his royalties by a lake and a large dam. His two companions were made vice ministers and given villas with small but shapely pavilions. The pig with a harem of human damsels. Of the naïve monk, of him, his piety and sincerity, no more has been heard. Gifted by the Buddha with foresight, he asked to be retired to the distant, walled-off Monastery of the Original Faith of Equal Austerity. There, at least, he breathes clean air.

The last trip to China was in 2015 with the Centre for Rising Powers and Global Development, under Dr. Jing Gu at the Institute of Development

Studies at Sussex, the institute founded by Dudley Seers and Hans Singer,[15] who had befriended me many years before. I haven't been to the country since. Hardening Chinese responses to the Tibetan issue, the Uighur issue, and latterly toward the youth of Hong Kong, have made it an unattractive destination for me. Head-hunters twice asked to put my name forward for the presidencies of Hong Kong universities, and I twice refused, saying that I would last five minutes the instant Beijing put pressure on the students—for I would, of course, defend my students. But on this last trip, the IDS delegation was hosted by the think tank attached to the prime minister's State Council, and, finally, I saw evidence of high-level research and thought toward Africa. Times had changed. They were now, in fact, quite sophisticated. But, by then, China's modality of approaching Africa had moved, as outlined earlier, more greatly toward a banking model. Whether this would help Africa or be a slow but sure replication of the Washington model is a key question. Certainly, significant indebtedness to China is piling up.

While seeking to remain even handed I had already begun to ask very public questions of Chinese policy and self-justifications, including on a much-watched programme on al-Jazeera.[16] It began to occur to me that in years to come, in any case, I would not be the most welcome guest in the land of my ancestors. That is the reality of it all. And I have not tried to hide my support for the Hong Kong students, from the Yellow Umbrella movement to the events of the present day. The difference from Tienanmen Square, revealing that the Chinese authorities do learn, is a replacement of tanks with slow, squeezing, and relentless suffocation. Or, they do not learn, but instead they use different, even if more patient, techniques to achieve the same end. The goal is aways the same. Under Heaven there is only variation but never change.

"Everyone Writes Otherwise"

Everyone writes otherwise. They send photographs.
St. Helen's Hospital. Ponsonby. Not far from the
view of blue harbour. Your first view of Auckland
before concrete buildings rose. I say, no. It was
by a thorn tree. Half Chinese, half African. My
mother alone delivered me, the swords and cudgels
of her rebel's art surrounding me. The first thing
my child's hand grasped was a bow of black horn.
They send me birth certificates, a doctor's
signature. Documents to live by. But my mother
wrapped me in a sable's pelt. She watched mist
rise in the mountains. Daily her hopes of
insurrection grew, sun flashing off the blades

she worked each morning. Noiselessly. She said
the forces of government hear everything, can see
nothing. I never cried. There were villages in the
mountains. Men and women were ceasing work. It was
like a litany. We are no longer content to be
labourers of the King. They would all die in the
summer uprising. An old man with white beard
carried me clear of the ambushes. I grew up.
My only heirlooms the bow of black horn, a sword
that fitted my hand if first I filled it with
spirit. I wake in the mornings, my mother inside the
sun. I send back the letters. I send back the
photographs. I know nothing of those blue harbours.
I let no one complain. But look in my eyes.
What vision of sunrise is imprinted there?
Not an arrow have I notched to the bow. But
when it filled the hand of my mother, it sang
of thirst and hunger. Its thirst and hunger.
Singing it would satisfy itself. A new day
breaks. Listen: I breathe
only what is true. The ancient Kings of this
continent took as thrones carved ebony and ivory.
Even now they rule. And where they sit
are rooted thrones of blood.[17]

NOTES

1. This has lasted to an appreciable extent. See Megha Mohan, "How George Floyd's Death Changed My Chinese Students," BBC, https://www.bbc.co.uk/news/stories-53208274, 29 June 2020.

2. Rana Mitter, *China's War with Japan, 1937–1945: The Struggle for Survival*, London: Allen Lane, 2013.

3. Gwyneth Williams, *Third World Political Organizations*, London: Macmillan, 1987, pp 52–53.

4. Stephen Chan, *Issues in International Relations: A View from Africa*, London: Macmillan, 1987, chapter 5.

5. Stephen Chan, "A Chinese Political Sociology in Our Times," *International Political Sociology*, 3:3, 2009, pp 332–334.

6. He was African Union chairman and president of the UN General Assembly's 59th session: https://www.un.org/en/ga/president/59/, 23 July 2020. Jean Ping, *And Africa Will Shine Forth: A Statesman's Memoir*, New York: International Peace Institute, 2012.

7. Yoon Jung Park, *A Matter of Honour: Being Chinese in South Africa*, Johannesburg: Jacana, 2008.

8. Related to me by survivors/veterans of 1955 on my visits to Kliptown in the first decade of the 2000s, when I would frequent the community center where they congregated.

9. Stephen Chan, "Ten Caveats and One Surmise in Our Contemplation of China and Africa," in Chris Alden, Daniel Large, and Ricardo Soares de Oliveira (eds.), *China Returns to Africa: A Rising Power and a Continent Embrace*, London: Hurst, 2008, pp 339–348.

10. Stephen Chan, "Untruthful Mandarins and Mandarins of Truth," *Focus*, 72, 2014, pp 60–63.

11. Chester Crocker, *High Noon in Southern Africa: Making Peace in a Rough Neighbourhood*, New York: W. W. Norton, 1993.

12. For my account of it and those of other members of the African delegation, see Stephen Chan (ed.), *The Morality of China in Africa: The Middle Kingdom and the Dark Continent*, London: Zed, 2013, and the report of the Brenthurst Foundation and its partners, https://www.cfr.org/report/africa-china-us-trilateral-dialogue, 2007.

13. Paul Moorcraft, *Inside the Danger Zones: Travels to Arresting Places*, London: Biteback, 2010, p 397.

14. In fact, on this visit I had for a time a ministerial black Lincoln and chauffeur/bodyguard/minder. The privileges, the car being sighted, were immense and immediate.

15. Stephen Chan, "A Brief History of Development Studies: An International Relations That Goes, Both Rightly and Wrongly, Where International Relations Dares Not Go," *European Review of International Studies*, 3:1, 2016, pp 93–104.

16. See the YouTube video available at the following: https://www.youtube.com/watch?v=F821Fe2_wBk&list=PLPp1F7IFcKeDlKUEdzv8-bX7rTJU5Y76e&index=8&t=0s, accessed 19 September 2014.

17. From Stephen Chan, *Crimson Rain*, Lampeter: Mellen, 1991.

Chapter 7

Facing the Tragedy of Our Days

The Israeli–Palestinian divide is one of the tragic ironies of our times—with emphasis on the tragedy. It is ironic, of course, because in living memory a people sought relief from mass persecution and the loss of rights. Sometimes the diplomatic contours that seek to police but not resolve this divide verge on tragi-comedy. I became directly involved as a result of the Brenthurst Foundation's initiative on insurgencies, following its established methodology of meeting in three cities.[1] One of the cities was Jerusalem and the unified delegation included generals from three countries, recent ambassadors and, once again, a smattering of "worldly" scholars. The Jerusalem leg in 2010 was hosted at the Menachim Begin Centre, and the key meeting involved an impressive and astounding briefing from the Israeli deputy prime minister Dan Meridor, number two at that time in an early Netanyahu government. He was meant to be the "dove" in the cabinet, although, as the U.S. general said to me, "If that's a dove, I hesitate to imagine the hawks."

I had already helped host in London the Palestinian Parliamentarian, Hanan Ashrawi—the boldly independent female legislator who, all the same, although hugely articulate, did not seem to have a coherent policy program. The usual demands of the Israelis and the West were there. But, in my role as rapporteur to her public address in 2004, I had to put her points into some sort of logical framework. That sort of framework continues to elude the Palestinian leadership, of which Ashrawi was often[2] critical—as was the intellectual hero of my young manhood, Edward Said.[2] I later found that the leaderships of neighbouring Arab states were also critical, as were the educated youth of Palestine.

I am deeply critical of Israeli expansionism. They too have no coherent policy as to what to do with a Palestinian population deprived in the future both of land and of rights. Endless suppression is not a workable policy. And I note the carefully orchestrated Israeli techniques—highly successful and deliberate—of labelling all critics of expansionism as anti-Semitic. But I also note many Jewish intellectual voices who are critics of expansionism.[3] On neither the Israeli nor Palestinian governmental sides is there an intellectual and politically ethical framing of the future involving two equal peoples—whether or not there are two states. But the two-state "solution" is probably dead anyway, so the framing has to be with status, rights, and citizenship in a single state with equalities in rights, including rights to ownership. Finally, it comes down, as illustrated here, to a ruthlessness in things physical and material in a tiny space.

But the issue of how seriously or otherwise the Palestinian leadership was taken by other Arab states was driven home to me at the height of the Arab Spring. In 2012, the British Council convened a private conference of the Ministers of Higher Education, and several university presidents, from the Middle East and North Africa (MENA) region, in Mohammedia, Morocco, not far from Casablanca. I was invited to address the gathering on the subject of why highly educated young people were protesting in their countries. I had already co-hosted a delegation of Moroccan university presidents at SOAS on the same theme. As is usual at all such conferences, each minister had to present a position paper on higher education in their own country. The Jordanian minister gave a bravura performance, with immaculate data, extrapolated and projected forward across every aspect of university performance. He was either himself a technocrat or had mastered his brief superbly. We had been sitting together in the heavily guarded conference chamber, and I congratulated him when he came to sit down. Then the Palestinian minister got up to speak, and the audience of his peers began a barely repressed giggle. I asked my Jordanian friend why this was so. "Stephen, just listen when he speaks. He will say nothing. Nothing at all. He will have no data or worthwhile information to report. You will see he is here simply for the ride. Everyone in this room knows that." So it was he gave a vacuous speech, waving his arms about to emphasise and illustrate very little. By comparison with the other speeches, it was appalling.

In 2010, at the Brenthurst meeting in Jerusalem, we had very little leeway to have anything to do with the Palestinians. We had weaved in and out of the incomplete wall the Israelis were building as we drove to Jerusalem from Ben Gurion Airport outside Tel Aviv. The driver had picked me up, along with a former British ambassador. As we veered to the Palestinian side of the wall, my companion asked the driver, "What would we do if we were attacked?" The driver pulled out a Glock pistol. My colleague asked, "Oh, do you know how to use that?" At that point, seated beside the driver, I turned and gave one of those "shut up" expressions instantly recognized by diplomats. It was the pistol issued to the execution squads in the 2009 attack on Gaza. Well, we were to be the guests of the "dovish" deputy prime minister, so it was perhaps inevitable we would have been picked up by a plain-clothes military officer.

But the deputy prime minister, fully cognizant that he should not bluff and bluster in front of a group of generals (the British general had just come out of being second in command of the multinational forces in Iraq) and ambassadors, had prepared an extraordinarily detailed and fully candid briefing (which in the end lasted longer than scheduled) on the history of the land-for-peace negotiations between the two sides. Detailed maps with colored lines (which I kept, smuggling them out of the room) revealed the positions of each of the long series of negotiations—none of them successful. Afterward, he assigned a colonel to oversee a small bus that took us to see the lines in their actuality. We were standing on a windswept hill when the U.S. general suddenly gripped me by the arm: "Stephen, those lines in negotiation x, that's what we can see below us now. They're only as far apart as a football field! And they couldn't agree!" But that was it precisely. The country/countries is/are tiny. A properly marshalled armoured division should have been able to cut it in half in an hour. That successive Arab armies failed to do so speaks not only to Israeli military elan and capacity, but to utter Arab military incompetence and ineptitude.[4]

But, on that visit, wandering the streets at night, I became deeply familiar with the old city of Jerusalem. It's the Ottoman city. The daytime American religious tourists, hauling (balsa wood) crosses to emulate Jesus on the Via Dolorosa and imagining they are in the city as it was in His time, are being ignorant and ridiculous. That city was destroyed by the Romans in 70 AD, and the dispersal of the rebellious population led to the 2,000-year era of the "Wandering Jew." But tourism earns money, and the Israelis welcome the visitors and foster the impersonation. If it looks old, surely it must be old. Yes? But not all is as it seems in this troubled region, and the taking of sides is often the adoption of stripped-down simplicities.

But I wanted to see and hear the Palestinian side of things as well. That chance came in 2012 with an invitation to be that year's Kenyon Institute Lecturer, in association with the British Council, delivering lectures in a number of Palestinian cities, starting with East Jerusalem—theoretically Palestinian territory, starting opposite the Damascus Gate of the old city, whence St. Paul by legend set off to persecute the Christians in Damascus, before his own conversion in an attack of blinding light. Directly opposite the Gate is the Nablus Road. The British Council, whose own offices were near that road fought shy, at the last moment, of housing me in the Colony, a grand hotel—an entire floor of which was occupied at $2 million per year by Tony Blair in his masquerade as a Middle East mediator. Since I had written an entire book on problems surrounding the Iraq War, in which throughout I had refused to use his name, referring to him only as the British prime minister[5] not I who will write his name into history—it was better I did not run into him. So I stayed instead in a more modest but pleasing hotel in the same road, opposite the Palestinian Pottery, where the most wonderful work from Hebron was on display.[6] Of Hebron, more later.

Carrying British Council papers helped me get through Ben Gurion Airport, where any hint of Palestinian involvement normally shuts down or hampers entry; and driving with British diplomatic number plates meant immunity at roadblocks—but more than once I asked my driver to drive through and wait on the other side while I joined the queue of Palestinians being checked by sometimes appallingly young Israeli conscripts, male and female, who did, to be fair, merely laugh at me. Once, after having been deposited by my driver in Nablus for my lecture, I took the public bus back to Jerusalem and, again to be fair, suffered not so much harassment as constant delays. But if I had to go through that every day, simply by virtue of being Palestinian, I would hardly be greatly pro-Israeli, and certainly not if I were an older person, seeking the dignity age is meant to confer, with my right of passage in the hands of someone younger than my sons and daughters. Winning hearts and minds is not a great Israeli project, and, of course, it cannot ever be a successful one without a programme of rights and equalities. Without that, the idea of justice is lost from the outset. You cannot pat nicely on the head a subjugated people.

This is a difficult situation. The Jewish people faced with being wiped out in a single foul swoop will take traumas into succeeding generations. And, of course, imperial settlements have much to be regretted or reflected upon in the aftermath. But international recognitions of statehood being what they are, the failure of international recognition is precisely toward a Palestinian state—and, as I said earlier, this is now unlikely. So the hypotheses, usually somewhat fanciful, are to do with best contingencies. On this visit, I had dinner with the Berkeley-trained (to PhD level) Palestinian Christian mayor of Bir Zeit, a town with shared Palestinian and Israeli control. Of that, more later, but his other guests were a cosmopolitan cast, including a Japanese/Palestinian opera singer. I have retained her CD. Her high notes are too shrill, but the lyrics of her longing, and that of the Palestinian composer, for a just settlement are so substantial that one forgives technique for a terrifying reality.

The first is how to remain calm, even as a middle-class person, in the face of constant degradation. By that I mean the constant adjustment to the fact that one has few employable rights. The second is that, even as a mayor, one's ability to represent one's constituents and community can be procedurally dense—so one must keep trying—but it's finally futile. The third is that, precisely by being middle class, one can relocate to the Gulf States, to Abu Dhabi or Qatar, but that would stick in the craw of abandoning one's country people. The fourth is that one has the wherewithal to invest in economic initiatives (e.g., olive oil from olive trees owned for generations by Palestinian families), only to have those plantations seized. And the fifth is to have children at university who participate in student councils, and who are then placed into never-ending administrative detention without trial for advocating a student resolution to oppose occupation. If these are middle class concerns of everyday life and thought that seek, even assiduously, to avoid the "big" questions of twin state/one state/historical right or wrong, I hesitate to imagine life at the far end of a class scale that exists in Palestine as anywhere else.

Some at least of this I saw in Hebron, a bitterly and literally divided city with Israeli settlers occupying the more modern part, the old town still in Palestinian hands but with American Jewish youngsters, gap-year shock troops as it were, squatting in the top floors of buildings overlooking narrow streets and deliberately tipping their faeces onto passers-by. International monitors, with no powers to do anything but monitor, told me that school children were a favourite target. I was able to cross over onto settler territory and saw almost every adult carrying Uzi assault weapons. The rate of fire of an Uzi is the fastest in the world and they made this wild west frontier somewhat more potentially violent than anything with six guns—or anything, if push came to shove, that Palestinian militias could muster with AK47s. In a word, they would be totally outgunned. From Nablus to Hebron, street murals of heroic Palestinian fighters belied the reality of one-sided fire fights and defeat.

I crossed over through the tomb of Abraham, a founding father to both nations, and ironically the dividing line of both nations in Hebron, my papers checked by Falasha conscripts whose parents had been rescued from Ethiopia many years earlier. I did think, ruefully, that if I had after all ridden shotgun for those convoys of evacuation to the Promised Land, then it would have been the children of those I helped rescue who were challenging me with their firepower. I'm very used to this, but someone always has his gun trained on you as you slowly hand over your papers. But I found the Palestinian sniper's nest used in the last militarised standoff between the two communities. If you play football with the children in the streets, despite the fact that you are awaiting a knee operation which made every trick shot painful, they will take you to meet their parents and the parents will tell you stories and take you to the scenes of struggle. A grand view of Hebron from the only once sniper's nest. Now overlooked by an Israeli watchtower.

And the knee was made worse as, some kilometres outside Bethlehem on the way back from Hebron, I fell off a cliff as I was craning for a better appreciation of the intended route of the Israeli wall—right through Palestinian vineyards, making access to one half of those vineyards almost impossible. But, before reaching that point, we had enjoyed lunch with the freshest of salads in a rural restaurant. The table next to mine was filled with American nuns come to tour the Holy Land. Two days later, I learned, the restaurant was demolished by Israeli bulldozers. I have a photograph, sent to me, of the distraught owner standing amidst the wreckage of his business. It was not strategically placed in any way. No possible "terrorist" use could have been made of it. It was gratuitous. In the meanest of ways, the Israelis lose long-term international respect, even as they make short-term gains. It seemed almost as if a nation that was once brutally terrorised can't get over the kick and thrill of being able to do the same. This, as well as the despairing trauma of the Holocaust, may be part of the psychological legacy of a nation born from wars and genocide.

On that visit I was intrigued by the standard of the students I addressed at the University of Nablus. The lecture was on a topic entirely unrelated to local issues—on the relationship between China and Africa—as an attempt to make the Kenyon Lectures non-parochial and cosmopolitan. But the students were not ignorant of problems beyond their location and asked intelligent questions as an extraordinarily well-behaved audience. As I was to find later at Bir Zeit University, they only had to get used to you and robust debate would certainly occur. And visiting tenure at Bir Zeit, the most prestigious of the Palestinian universities, was what came next in 2015, when I was appointed Konrad Adenauer Foundation Chair of Academic Excellence at the university. Following the U.S. model of three-hour lecture/seminars, and doing this almost every day to condense a semester into the shorter time I had available, allowed me to know my students, 80 percent of them female, well. They were extremely bright. It was a master's class in international diplomacy.[7] Most would have done well in my master's classes at SOAS. The Islamic girls flirted by showing me cell-phone pictures of themselves without hijab on their hair; the Christian girls by waving their hair around during class. For me, defusing this was easy. I just waved my hair around in reply. The hilarity set the scene for some very intense lectures and discussions.

But it was also a very politicised class. Despite being the length of the country away from the Hamas strongholds, the student body had overwhelmingly voted Hamas in the Student Council elections—entirely, they told me, as a protest vote against the PLO, which they regarded as corrupt, nepotistic, and bereft of new ideas. One of the young students was a newlywed—for the girls marry young, sexual relations being deeply frowned upon before marriage—and her husband was in administrative detention for organizing a protest against occupation. There is no trial, and detention can be extended indefinitely. I observed that they were building a McDonald's restaurant in downtown Ramallah, a short walk from where I was lodged in the Trade Tower—a Chinese-built monstrosity that towered over that part of town without any sense of perfect working order. "So, they said, we shall be a prison with a McDonald's." This said with such spite that I had to reflect long upon its provenance. And this became clear to me on a long drive to Bethlehem, to be the guest of the family of one of my colleagues. With Israeli papers we should have covered the distance in far less than one hour. Without such papers, we had to take a circumlocution around Jerusalem that took more than two hours, on a new road with billboards that proudly proclaimed it had been built by U.S. AID. So it is to be a comfortable prison, complete with scenic route and hamburgers. All trimmings courtesy of the United States. Everything but rights. And I had a very good look at what looked to be Dodge Ram trucks, painted Khaki, with extended trays, provided by the United States to the Palestinian defence forces. Very pretty, but with no armour. In fact, given that my high window overlooked the defence force headquarters, I could count exact numbers of vehicles, patrol times, numbers of men in the barracks, and so forth. Security was appalling and amateurish. I would pretend to be lost and ask, as if they were London policemen, Palestinian officers for directions. Too startled to bully me, they struggled with their English while I inspected every inch of their weaponry. Everything, like hamburgers in Ramallah, flattered to deceive. None of it could have effect in any remotely serious situation. A lightly armed parade ground army that, even so, President Trump ceased to fund. I spoke to those close to the U.S. commanding officer of the military aid mission. Ensuring it looked pretty but was several notches below what the Israelis had was precisely the name of the game. And, on that visit to Bethlehem, I was taken to see the family's generations-old olive tree plantation—which had just been seized by the Israelis.

"At Bethlehem"

There was a saviour.
A church has crushed the manger.

King of the Jews
And of all the Jews survey.

Surveyors build a wall
Crush the Promised Land.

When the land was wise
Solomon loved a Shulamite

A Palestinian maid
With breasts like turtledoves. [8]

The vexed politics of it all became abruptly clear one night in Ramallah's most exclusive restaurant. It was Ramadan and we were waiting for the priest's prayer at sunset that signalled permission to eat. This usually also signalled a stampede for the buffet. People grow fat in the month of penance.

But, while waiting, my interpreter suddenly began speaking to me in French. I responded in kind. But he signalled with his eyes to the table behind ours, and said in French, "The four commanders of the Palestinian intelligence service. They think we can't understand them. You can't. I can. They are plotting the overthrow of the leadership of the Palestinian authority. I will interpret for you in French. I'm sure they won't understand that we understand."

Ramadan carried with it certain privileges. The chef of my hotel and I had become friends. I would teach him how to cook Chinese for his visitors from Beijing. He, in return, fed me the most wonderful mezze with the freshest ingredients. But, one night, in the hotel's revolving restaurant, the waiters came to me with a pitcher of red liquid. "Dr. Stephen, we know you are not a believer, but you have tried so hard to observe our customs. You will see that the other diners are drinking tamarillo juice. It is a Ramadan practice. You will see it is the color of wine. Therefore, each night, but in a tamarillo glass, we shall bring you wine to thank you for trying to be with us. No one will know." A tamarillo glass is larger than a wine glass. Thus it is that the guerrilla of solidarity may still observe his own French habits in a land of distress and piety.

One day, before my pickup for lectures, I was walking the streets of Ramallah when I spied my SOAS student, Phoenix, who was taking a post-graduation gap year and enjoying the Ramallah underground gay and lesbian club scene. We embraced in the streets, bringing the sparse traffic to a halt. She was on her way to a protest against Israeli intrusions and the surge of occupations in East Jerusalem, but when I questioned her about the night-clubs, she laughed. "Stephen, you'd be so out of place. From ten miles away you are as straight as a spirit level." So, despite my best efforts, not all of modern Palestinian culture came within my experience. But gay, straight, male, female, Islamic, Christian, the young people I met and taught were magnificently resilient. But they all saw they had no future in Palestine with both relentless encroachment of the occupation and an inept and self-serving Palestinian authority. From my windows I could see the president's new palace being built on the neighbouring hills. As ever, in such lands, the priorities are toward the elite. Nearby, on a slightly more distant hill, was a new city under construction—with Israeli encouragement—for the rich Palestinian diaspora that might be induced home. The Israelis even finessed the supply of water—something perennially used as a weapon against the Palestinians. Ramallah would stay "free"-ish and that came to mind when I again met up with the mayor of Bir Zeit. He picked me up in his vintage Mercedes and, because he was Christian, we were able to drink wine in his garden before sunset.

"What will they leave us, Stephen?"

"They will leave you a necklace of 'free' cities, possibly with link roads in place of contiguity. They will come to own everything else. In effect, a necklace of free ghettos, some highly reduced hinterland around the cities, and everywhere surrounded by an easily militarised Israeli presence. Your being spread out with roads that can be cut off, means you will never be able to mobilise a securitised response, even in your own self defence. And they will never allow you to have an airport."

He opened another bottle of wine. The call to prayer blasted out from the neighbourhood minaret. "I recorded the decibels," he said, "it's louder than a rock concert."

I have not written to him to ask if he recognized my prediction in the Trump peace plan for Israel and Palestine. For that is exactly what much of the "free world" sees as a just solution for the great tragedy caused by Western civilization. It may indeed recognise certain realities on the ground—occupation has been very successful—but it is hardly just.

I had very much wanted, however, to include in my lecture series a detailed presentation of the Israeli case. I invited two Israeli friends to come up from Jerusalem to hear it. They were terrified crossing into so-called Palestinian territory. But I had briefed the university guards to let through, with utmost politeness, the car bearing Israeli number plates; similarly asking the reception desk in the Faculty of Law building to usher in my guests; and briefing my students to exhibit the courtesies of their culture. Everyone behaved flawlessly. However, you could have heard a pin drop while I lectured over two full hours, giving immense detailing of each stage of my argument. This side of things is not often presented in Palestine, just as the Palestinian side is not often presented in the halls of Israeli academe and certainly not in the Israeli Knesset or parliament.

I spoke on the historical timelines since antiquity. Not quite as extensive as Jewish and Christian fundamentalists maintain. On the release from Babylonian captivity by a Persian king—in today's terms, an Iranian. On the destruction of Jerusalem in 70 AD, the Roman dispersal of the population, and the era thereafter of the "wandering Jew." On the early formation of Orthodoxy as a gesture of pride in the ghettos of Europe. On the early formations of Zionism and the hopes of Herzl. On the Balfour Declaration and how I had frequented the same room in the Reform Club where, by legend, the document was given Rothschild. On the Holocaust. On how the transition, after the war, from British to UN control was mishandled. On the birth of Jewish terrorism to hasten the process of independence. On the Palestinian fighting response and the flight to which it led in what is called the Nakba. On each of the four great Arab–Israeli wars and the military strategies used by the Israelis to be triumphant in each—albeit with almost a tank-on-tank stalemate on the Golan Heights against Syrian forces before Israeli aerial strength turned the tide. On the early idealism of the kibbutz movement. On successive Israeli governments up to Netanyahu. On what the Israeli scholar, Uriel Abulof, calls an existential dread of Jews one day being outnumbered by Palestinians—with no rights and great resentments.[9] Of the Jewish scholars who had objected to expansionism after the Oslo Accords. On those Accords themselves. And, drawing from Meridor's briefing some years earlier, on the stages of the doomed land-for-peace negotiations. And how, in the wake of no capacity in the Netanyahu government to imagine any possible compromise, the policy of expansion and suppression was adopted as default. I concluded by relating my prediction to the mayor of Bir Zeit, host town to Palestine's most prestigious university—that there will be only a necklace left. But that posterity will judge how righteous or otherwise Israel was, with whatever rue that history might bequeath.

I then asked my Israeli visitors if I had been fair. One was himself a professor who had never before been in a lecture room with Palestinian students. Yes, it was fair.

I added a postscript that the Palestinian Authority was not exactly covering itself with glory in its international representation of itself, relating the reception accorded the minister of higher education by his peers. At this, the students also sniggered. They knew this man well. Partly because of him they had felt driven to vote Hamas in their student council elections.

When the lecture series was over, I asked my students what their plans might be. "We shall go to the Gulf. There is nothing for us here." But they had talent which one side would repress and their own side ignore. At least the Gulf States had McDonald's without the hamburgers seeming like prison food. They write to me from the Gulf that at least the surrounding seas make life seem less imprisoned. But even the Gulf States had their own problems.

"Sheba"

She came with cages of doves
proud and
        as her reputation promised
        beautiful
        but scathing in her knowledge
        of all things.

Knowing more languages than even Solomon
including the tongues of the fish.
For, as she said to him,
        You merely passed through.
        I swam the Red Sea
        in all its reaches

and learned from
the Ghost of Ramses
amidst his rusted chariots
about the dupes of history.
Even Ramses was the Tool of God.

He looked on her.
She was like the Shulamite.
Had she come to taunt him?

But Sheba smiled and said
As a gesture of peace
between wise people
I have come to release the doves.

I took the long way round getting to the Gulf, noting tensions among the countries there, but also noting how certain of them were carefully developing roles as mediatory or facilitating entities in international relations. The model, it seemed to me, was almost drawn from Helsinki in the Cold War era. Certainly, the Doha round of trade negotiations, established for many years in Qatar, depicted a facilitating role in international economic relations. The harder forms of political international relations were always there, awaiting a prompt.

There were symbolic dress rehearsals that spoke to the balancing acts these small but rich countries had constantly to perform. During Gulf War One, from 1990 to 1991, I was a visiting professor in Geneva, teaching at graduate level a class entirely composed of diplomats and international civil servants. One of my students was the ambassador of Qatar, and Qatar was a member of the coalition of armed forces fighting alongside NATO armies to liberate Kuwait from Saddam. Kuwait being their neighbour, this meant something to them. It also meant their being used. To lay down a signal at least to delay being used and abused in the future, even the Syrians sent an army contingent. But one night, after a prolonged U.S. bombardment of Saddam's lines, the ambassador called on me with a bottle of whiskey. I said, "You're not allowed to drink." His reply was, "Tonight, please teach me, for the land invasion to retake Kuwait begins tonight. Not led by the Americans. For symbolism obviously, the cynical nature of which I understand, but which all the same I appreciate, the spearhead will involve Qatari troops. It will be on CNN."

As indeed it was—the location having been quite obviously cleared beforehand by probably non-Qatari troops (the Qatari army had not previously seen action anywhere)—under floodlights, with Qatari armoured cars painted white, and with CNN cameras mounted on them. I sighed and said to the ambassador, "Look, with whiskey—and, by the way, your driver is waiting outside to ensure you get home, yes?—you start by smelling the aroma and then by some judicious and polite rotation within your mouth, appreciating the taste, before you slowly swallow. The taste will be discerned by your mouth, not your throat. You got that?" I helpfully drank most of the bottle myself. He had, after all, to be a functioning diplomat, not to mention my functioning student, the next day. It was, appallingly, Chivas Regal. I have no idea why Americans, Indians, Middle Easterners, and Eastern Europeans, including Russians, think Chivas is a good whiskey. Philistines, one and all . . .

As the years passed, I began accepting invitations to speak in Turkey, long a favourite if problematic country for its historical and contemporary role as a crossroads, both literally and culturally. Every tension was there and for the most part, amazingly, transacted throughout history without ethnic or confessional genocides. I was to become a regular speaker at the annual Istanbul security conference. At these events giving your paper, even if it is a keynote, is not the point. The point is being invited to private side-discussions. This is where messaging occurs—Turkish views inflected via means of imparting confidential information. It comes via networks and third parties. I was taken aside by an Egyptian general and offered a chance to hear the tapes of the 2018 Khashoggi assassination, the terrifyingly botched Saudi murder on Turkish soil. I listened to the pleas of a leader of the Free Syrian Army, knowing only too well the very members of his small audience would betray him with treachery piled upon treachery. As we parted, the Free Syrian spokesman said to me, "I hope we shall meet again, *Inshallah*." I replied, "*Inshallah*," but confident the bullet with his name on it was already being prepared.

Learning how to behave at such occasions had begun with the Halifax Security Conference in 2011. Often referred to as the NATO "Davos," this one was intent upon celebrating victory over Gadaffi's Libya. In front of 300 gentlemen, and a small smattering of gentle women, all wearing generals' stars on their epaulets (except the Canadians, who wore maple leaves . . .) I stood up and said that I didn't fully understand the air of victory. "After all, a desert army of mercenaries stood their ground for six months before everything NATO air power could throw at them. They never broke and ran." I never did get invited back to Halifax, but I was there in the first place because it had become known that I had advised the Libyan opposition as it rose up in Benghazi.

One of my adventuring but brilliantly capable students had wound up as special assistant to a key Libyan rebel leader stationed in the United Arab Emirates. So it was one day, with Gadaffi's tanks at the gates of Benghazi, and with the dictator's son speaking portentously of rivers of blood, promising them, that my phone rang.

"The French have offered to recognize us."

"If I were you, I'd accept the French offer right away."

"We do wish to, but we need your help. We don't want the French to think we are barbarians and so wish to reply in proper formal diplomatic language."

"How much time do you have?"

"They are awaiting an answer as we speak."

"It's going to be in English. I can't do it in perfect diplomatic French at this short notice. I'm going to dictate it down the phone now . . ."

As for what happened afterward, my involvement snowballed but cannot even now be much discussed. Suffice to say that if the great powers had rolled Gaddafi back from Benghazi, then facilitated negotiations for a federal Libya, the terrible cataclysm caused by regime change without a plan may have been avoided. Everyone expected Gaddafi's mercenary army of Mauritanians, Chadians, and others to melt away at the first NATO bombardment. As I said in Halifax, they stood and fought pretty much every inch of the way. All chaos was sowed in the slipstream of the cruise missiles and fighter bombers.

The fight was, in fact, region-wide. Much of the Libyan rebellion was planned and directed from the United Arab Emirates. Benghazi fighters used Egyptian band widths when Gaddafi tried to close Libyan cyber space to them. But U.S. regional power and influence were greatly enhanced and ties with Saudi Arabia as a lynchpin ally were consolidated. This did not cause joy for Iran or for those hoping that there could be a negotiated way forward for the tensions between Saudi Arabia and Iran. And, if they got rid of Gaddafi, the temptation was wide open to contemplate a getting rid of the Ayatollah's Iran.

Because Qatar thought it only sensible to maintain diplomatic channels with Iran, allowing itself to be a conduit for diplomacy, it earned the wrath of a newly confident and self-righteous Saudi Arabia—not even knowing how many mistakes it was committing: war in Yemen, the assassination of Khashoggi, and then the blockade of Qatar. The blockade was very much punishment for Qatarian diplomacy toward Iran. The aim was, literally, to starve Qatar into submission, blockading land borders and closing Saudi airspace to flights bound for Qatar. A huge amount of Qatari imports of food and essential commodities came via or over Saudi Arabia. The Saudis thought they could bring Qatar to its knees in two weeks.

The Qatari response was to appoint a small number of highly technocratic young men to work basically anyone in the world who would listen in the search of alternative supplies and transport routes. They worked pretty much around the clock, broke the blockade, and ruefully mentioned to me afterward that Qataris only complained of not always having their favourite brands. But no one went without.

Qatar is a far from perfect society but, at the 2018 Istanbul Security Conference, one of the respondents to my keynote was the woman who was spokesperson, now deputy minister, for the Qatari Ministry of Foreign Affairs. She asked me to come to Qatar to appraise how they had done in running and breaking the blockade.

It was one of those slightly protocol-fussy visits. A white limousine awaited me on the tarmac. It drove me to the VIP lounge (it would in fact have been quicker to walk from the air-bridge directly to the lounge), and a black limousine transported me to my hotel in Doha where I had a balcony and superb view of the sea. It had been a long time since I had received the ambassadorial treatment—so I didn't complain. And, besides, it was too hot to walk in the Doha days, so I enjoyed my black limousine. I talked to the key executives who had planned and organized, and themselves conducted, the breaking of the blockade. None was older than their thirties. Throughout the government apparatus, the senior positions were filled by youthful and well-educated people. Mostly men. But I also noticed that when my female host in the Ministry of Foreign Affairs asked men to jump, they jumped. It was an intriguing few days.

I reported that the running of the blockade had been superb. That was basically what I had been brought to say—but it was true. It was a superb operation. And it kept the avenues of diplomacy open with Iran. I saw how that worked in late 2019, when I was invited to speak at the Doha Forum—probably the greatest diplomatic lovefest in the world where, again, the real business is done in secret bilaterals behind closed doors. I have no doubt that the superbly articulate Iranian minister of foreign affairs—who gave a finely crafted public speech—and the U.S. delegation, led by the secretary of the treasury, conspired to meet or exchange notes, despite the public antagonism caused by Donald Trump's repudiation of the nuclear agreement crafted by his predecessor's administration.[10]

I should make it clear that I am far from being supportive of government by ayatollahs. I believe in the secular state and the separation of church and state. However, I am also mindful of the ironies of history. It was Cyrus the Great, a Persian, who liberated the Jews from Babylon to rebuild their temple in Jerusalem and, under Ezra, begin the process of rewriting their history—which is the true foundation of the Old Testament today, not any earlier figure called Moses. The Cylinder of Cyrus was the first bill of human rights, promising religious freedom. Both today's Iranian ayatollahs, and today's Israeli government have forgotten the legacy of Cyrus: free religious diversity; and the foundations in codified written form of ancient Jewish history.

I am also very mindful of contemporary realities and how we have entered an epoch that draws from the one immediately before (i.e., we are in a new Cold War with clear trigger points in key regions of it becoming very hot). The suspicion that Saudi Arabia plays a double game of being both a U.S. ally while covertly funding organizations such as ISIS;[11] a Cold War with an economic manifestation in the struggle between the United States and China; and a Middle East where, like once in Europe, we see a struggle to establish and manipulate a balance of power with superpower allies arrayed on different sides.

Not history repeating itself so much as an apparent mimesis that in fact acquires new and deadly attributes of its own. What I saw once in Africa, as the superpowers lined up their allies—for the United States, the key ally was Apartheid South Africa—is being restructured into conflict in the Middle East. Not just Arab states against Israel, but Middle Eastern states arrayed against each other. Into this maelstrom, somehow, ambivalences hanging off my coattails, I seem now to be drawn.

NOTES

1. https://www.kas.de/en/web/israel/veranstaltungen/detail/-/content/promoting-state-building-managing-fault-lines-ii, 5 August 2020; the book that was written to consolidate principles emerging from the discussions is Jeffrey Herbst, Terence NcNamee, and Greg Mills, *On the Fault Line: Managing Tensions and Divisions within Societies*, London: Profile, 2012.

2. Albeit with ambivalence. See Tariq Ali, *Conversations with Edward Said*, London: Seagull, 2006, pp 78–83.

3. For example, Avi Schlaim. For a collection of his articles see https://www.theguardian.com/profile/avi-shlaim, 7 August 2020.

4. Sydney D. Bailey, *Four Arab–Israeli Wars and the Peace Process*, Houndmills: Macmillan, 1990.

5. Stephen Chan, *Out of Evil: New International Politics and Old Doctrines of War*, Ann Arbor: University of Michigan Press, 2005.

6. This pottery features in a key moment of my novel: Stephen Chan, *Bonded Brothers*, London: Nth Position, 2017, pp 71–72.

7. These became Stephen Chan, *Mediations on Diplomacy: Comparative Cases in Diplomatic Practice and Foreign Policy*, Bristol: E-IR, 2017. The later edition of these lectures when I was George Soros Chair of Public Policy at Central European University, then in Budapest, are available in filmed summaries: https://www.youtube.com/playlist?list=PLPp1F7lFcKeBFtJz4KBo_tuTPCGwW79bT.

8. Not previously published. The last lines are a riff from *The Song of Solomon*, where the king falls in love with a "Shulamite," probably in today's terms a Palestinian—as did Boaz with the "Moabite," Ruth, and Moses, who married the daughter of the priest of Midian, both Moabites and Midianites being precursors of today's Palestinians. The turtledoves are drawn from Solomon's highly sensual song to her.

9. Uriel Abulof, "Deep Securitization and Israel's 'Demographic Demon,'" *International Political Sociology*, 8:4, 2014, pp 396–415.

10. John Kerry, *Every Day Is Extra*, London: Simon & Schuster, 2018, chapter 18.

11. Even Henry Kissinger indicated so in his *World Order: Reflections on the Character of Nations and the Course of History*, London: Allen Lane, 2014, pp 134–142.

Chapter 8

The Academy and the International

I had intended a small selection of experiences and reflections to illustrate some simple points. My life has been somewhat more varied than what is represented here, and the more extreme adventures have been left out. Adventures like the following, which didn't turn out wrong,[1] but others that certainly did.

At the end of 2009, at the Commonwealth summit in Trinidad, attended also by the UN secretary-general and the French president, a brief moment of post-Ramphal importance for the Commonwealth, I was covering the event for BBC with Zeinab Badawi—but had noticed, as we drove in from the airport, a vast community screened off by a wall beside the motorway. The newspaper headlines told of a ghastly ritual murder and decapitation behind the wall—in the desperate sprawling slum of Port of Spain, a slum called Sea Lots. So, after we had completed filming, I went to Sea Lots. I had asked community workers if I could meet the gang leaders who had purportedly committed the murder. My BBC colleagues meanwhile went to the beach.

I arrived at Sea Lots accompanied by a businessman who was a member of the political opposition, and we were met by a community worker. I asked whether the gang leader would come. "You must go to him. He is waiting at the end of this straight street. You can see him standing, looking at you, from the centre of the road." On both sides of the street were young men with machetes, axes, and hatchets, pretending to be clearing undergrowth. About two dozen of them. Very muscular but unconvincing gardeners, clearly a gauntlet.

So I walked slowly forward, shaking hands or touching fists with each one of the "gardeners," bowing slightly, making myself seem foreign but not an immigrant. I was still wearing the blue dress shirt Zeinab had made me buy for the television show. But it was clearly important not to rush. I arrived before the leader. He smiled. I had passed his test. I said, "What can I do for you to make your Sea Lots a slightly better place?" He came with me back to the community centre and laid out a programme. I agreed to fund the Christmas dinner for all the children of the slum and for their grandparents. My colleague agreed to buy new wheelchairs for the wounded members of the gang. The gang leader would not accept responsibility for the murder, saying only there was gang warfare, but did say he would prevent murders of innocent people. It worked out well. It had every prospect of not working out well. I have no idea why I did this—except a truly visceral feeling that, with all the pomp and ceremony, grandeur and expense of so many heads of state and government in town, millions spent solely on a new flag pole to display the Trinidad and Tobago flag, that young citizens had been forgotten, screened off, did not exist. I think it was the sight of the wall screening them off, making them not exist. I refused to attend any of the receptions and didn't tell my BBC colleagues where I had gone until afterward. My colleague has continued to fund the Christmas dinners and writes to say that the mad longhaired Chinese gentleman is remembered. I'm glad. As I intimated, there were other occasions when being able to sprint faster than one year's entry from Tonga in the Commonwealth Games 100 metres was very helpful. These days, with a brace of cobalt knees, it is not advisable to try this. Perhaps I shall need to go into the slums with a mobility scooter.

Looking over the preceding chapters, they seem like "war stories" from the proverbial grandfather. I'm sure some colouring has entered their telling—one has to live with one's memories after all—but they are all true. None of the accounts is fictional. They are accounts of an effort to do, clumsily and often unsuccessfully, some good. What I was struck by in the discipline of International Relations as it adopted what must be regarded as a rough and ready continental philosophical bent was its preoccupation with what may be regarded as true—as opposed to good. Speaking "truth to power" was of course a huge driver behind the critical theory that emanated from Adorno and Horkheimer who escaped obliteration in Hitler's Holocaust—they noting only too presciently how the Nazis deployed philosophy and culture to substantiate the "truth" of their power. The "true truth" became a philosophical quest—but to the extent that power no longer understands the academic discourses and debates about a truth that has become a reification and a vocabulary-ridden rhetoric. And, of course, there is the irony of vogues for thinkers who served the Nazi cause—often very well. But, basically, "power" is very happy that thinkers ponder "truth" and speak it in a way that no one understands what ethical moment of truthfulness is at stake.

I used a number of my poems, most previously published, because it was part of my literary reputation that I was an engaged writer. Translating that engagement from early days as the firstborn son of a refugee family, to the wider world whose wars had exiled them, saw writing as a continuity. I have kept writing poetry but, in recent years have published sparsely—firstly concentrating on my novels and, secondly, not being profoundly impressed by poetry as a particularly competitive, because narrow, niche in a British literary scene that is simultaneously kitchen sink and ungroundedly celestial in its ambitions. But I kept writing because I wanted, above all, to have a body of work that was able to say that one could write the international in more than just the received scholarly and technical practitioner modes. I wanted also to say that in living the international, not just thinking it and writing it, one enters emotional cataclysms. Dead bodies and oppression are both sobering and pause for thought. "Why them? Why am I the one who escapes? By what right is choice mine and not theirs?"

"The Fire at the Crossroads of the Soul"

Even if we are blessed by the gods, he said,
there will be a day of reckoning,
the blessed are not spared that
but rather the scales are weighted more heavily
to compensate what we were given
so that the normal ease, perhaps free elegance
of our decisions
might be truly costed out in limbs and heads,
hearts and souls,
of all those whom we left behind or over-rode,
unknowingly brushed aside
in our image of how to act,
as if, as we sometimes thought,
it had no consequence,
that our light carelessness was only a style
with no grieving wake of bruised dolphins
who might themselves have sought to toss airily
in the assurance of destiny.
Listen, there will be a day,
a crossroads where those who took the long route
will arrive at last, their accusations fully listed,
and the gods will say "yes"
and the scales will be stood
two noose-hung filigrees of cause and effect
and the blue fire will melt
all our hologrammic, soul imposturing
sense of blessing.
We are men, he said, sailing towards stakes.

That these questions are largely ignored in an international relations that is for the most part no longer experiential, no longer praxiological, made it seem urgent to contribute this volume to this series.

My complaint is in part reminiscent of Edward Said's own in one of his parting works, *On Late Style*, where he recognises a certain anger in the late works of basically his heroes. Where did a lifetime of creating without anger get them? They are forgiven late anger.[2] Hidemi Suganami once told me that, every year, he re-reads Kenneth Waltz almost as a ritual to probe the mystery of his thought. I confess I re-read *On Late Style* every year to probe the mystery of anger while still creating and writing.

Nothing of this seeks to be self-righteous. All of my life was without any expectation of entitlement. Early poverty and continuing discrimination ensured that. Without sounding cliché, you accepted that you had to fight for what seemed important both to yourself and to your vision of the world. The discriminations were there to be risen above so that, in New Zealand, as the only person to have come second in the competitions for the Rhodes, Commonwealth, and Harkness Scholarships, one wondered if being Chinese had become that final line of not yet a crossing. The first Chinese New Zealander to win a Rhodes did so very recently. Fifty years ago was perhaps far too early. But when I entered university management and became the dean of humanities at Nottingham Trent University, with a war chest of funds to recruit talent to transform the faculty like a football manager transforms a football team, I was the only Chinese dean of a faculty of humanities in all of Europe. Chinese deans of business and engineering faculties to be sure—so at least the stereotypes were slightly more refined.

And I don't even mean to seem self-righteous about the preoccupations and serious research of my theoretical colleagues. I myself am fascinated by theory and have published papers on Paul Ricoeur, using Julia Kristeva, Lacan, Rorty, referencing Walter Benjamin, and doing so with the enthusiasm of the best of them.[3]

What I mean to say is that this cannot fully represent the international. Insofar as it becomes an armchair or library discipline, it cannot fully represent the international. The international is represented when the despair and anguish it contains is witnessed at close quarters and shared—even if one has the final plane ticket out. Looking down the barrel of a gun is at least a sharing of that moment with others. "Will he fire? Will he fire?" What color is the last sky?

I don't want to labour these points, but to illustrate them I conclude this book with two last poems. The first was written in the aftermath of questions and decisions that encroached upon me in 1982. One of them arose when, in Nairobi, on my way to Uganda to help rebuild the country shattered by Amin, the call from the Palestinian Liberation Organization reached me—seeking desperately to recruit an international brigade to help in the defence of Beirut. Since, among other things, I was to be involved in settling a little civil war in Uganda, it seemed that more than one war at a time was gilding the lily far too much. But it struck me afterward that I was probably one of the few people to have been the target for recruitment by both the PLO and Mossad. Attempting to be even-handed does lead to intriguing consequences. The consequences of many emotions felt meant that, for this book, I have provided some explanatory footnotes to this first poem. [4]

"A View from My Terrace"

If I say it now—yes, let me say it now,
the sounds of the city rising, having decided
to leave my employment, to leave this life
of hotel suites, Permanent Secretaries,
to shake off, above all, the institutional view,
to look at this life from afar—let me say
steam rises from my heart like the traffic
roar from the streets. East Africa's
largest circus, arteries snaking into
the suburbs, winding into River Road,[5]
leading to the Casino Kung Fu Cinema,
to the Hotel Solace, past crippled beggars,
to Nairobi's theatre—ageing expatriates
playing out second-hand memories of
Broadway hits.

I should say it nervously,
I should say it from my terrace,
but the traffic, the perfect cinematic
crescent kick, the Sondheim songs
remind me of another life. I came here.
It seemed appropriate.
This time in Nairobi, I am trying to
catch a plane. I am trying to overcome
the computer bookings. I say, I too
push keyboards. I write words.
Let your keyboard confirm my flight.

For everything has started.
Thousands of Palestinians stream
into Beirut. From all over the world.
They come to take part in the final stand.
The Madrid of our times. Here, from his

terrace, Colonel Berger/Malraux/Chan is
contemplating the traffic, is learning
about it all from Time and Newsweek.[6]
And feeling, here too, something is
building. Visit by visit, a palpable tension
builds.

What builds? The magazine sellers have
the latest Vogue, Gentleman's Quarterly.
The Dragon Pearl still serves the finest
won ton in Africa.[7] The Hilton Hotel
gymnasium is empty, awaiting my return.
Mary Wa Betty, her hair plaited, patrols
the same corner at night. Says to me, on
my regular sleepless rambles, would you like
to push my buttons?

I say, I am impotent, sick. Mary buys me
coffee. She too likes to talk, says,
something is rising in my heart of gold.

I am sitting at my terrace. In suite 409.
I am thinking about Brother Omondi. about
his ceaseless energy. About his tea and sugar
runs, late at night, for the parking boys of
the city.[8] Few yards from the Hilton, the
homeless huddle. Planners hatch complex schemes:
return the parking boys to their parents.
Brother Omo shows me first the boys,
then the parents. Exiles together, late, on
the streets of Nairobi. Buys the boys tea and
bread at the all-night café. I watch
each boy tip seven spoons of sugar into his tea.
I ask, where do you sleep? They say, there, there . . .

I am sitting at my terrace. My suite is full
of magazines. The junkie for gloss is back.
Omo is coming to take me, as he does on each
visit, training the soul, to the Mathare Valley,
to Kinyago: to walk through the lines of mud
shelters; to read the signs (Welcome to the
Mathare Valley Hotel), to be welcomed into houses
of stolen black plastic sheets. The children
remember me. I demonstrate for them kicks,
hyper-flexions, spins, hands faster than the eye
can see.

This time, I remove my shirt. Someone removes
his belt. Tense, nerveless, I demonstrate I too
can block out pain; I too am stoic; I can take it,
five minutes at a time.[9]

Omo's Madonna! How can all this continue!
Something is building. The cars seem more urgent.
Songs of love and clowns seem more grotesque than ever.

And I, Citizen Chan, am trying to catch
a plane to Uganda. His last mission. His back
unmarked. But listless, emptied of it all,
except this steamy feel inside his chest.
Omo, won't you ventilate my heart?
Won't you draw me back from my terrace?
Draw closed the sliding glass doors?
The heavy duty nylon weave curtains?
Press for me the muzak channel.
And order, please, some harmless drink
which tastes like dry straight gin
which (never mind the olive) kicks like a mule
but has no after-effects.

Tell Mary Wa Betty, please, to leave her corner.
I'll give her three hundred shillings to rub
These rock hard pectorals.

You should write a play about it.
Call it, the Mandarin's Concern.
Set in hotel suites, in endless plane journeys,
endless stopovers in Nairobi.
Yes, he has a friend. Washed white by the Lamb.
Neither of them flies to Beirut.
Both of them are endlessly polite to their
Jewish friends.
One of them would like to drive in the Safari
Rally.
Crash a Peugeot for Jesus.

Omo,
what introspection was being recorded
at the Kimani Court
while the rain was falling over Nairobi
while the students were asleep
unaware of their impending slaughter

and various other people were preparing moves
as old and ritualized
as any tragedy.[10]

As I mention in the opening chapter, Stuart Grief's Berkeley PhD thesis on the New Zealand Chinese had declared me as a rebel figure. This rebelliousness caused my family much grief. Later, my affiliation to African movements raised more eyebrows. Before then, when I was president of the national student body, the first ambassador of the People's Republic of China decided to host his first reception, and it was for my student body—as the key nongovernmental body that had agitated for "normalization" of relationships. This would have alarmed even more of my diasporic community who had unwaveringly supported the Kuomintang in Taiwan—and it is just as well that the drinking competition between me and the ambassador, of a rocket fuel called Mao Tai, did not become too public knowledge. I won, downing thirty-two shots of the noxious liquid that had done for Nixon when, in the same year of 1973, he and Kissinger had normalised relations in Beijing. I drove home along winding roads in the Wellington hills singing superb opera. It was for the sake of diplomacy . . . of course.

But all joking aside, neither parent is alive now to receive apologies and they never received a full explanation. This poem that concludes this book is an explanatory amends to their souls. [11]

"It Was Not Kindness That Brought Me Here"

It was not kindness that brought me here, but
Buddha's eight-fold path. One night I saw the
sun set in Mt. Roskill, from the terrace of my
father's home. He let me go, knowing the call
had come. I was not afraid. But climbing down
the stairs I did not know how, cunningly, the
country had rotted. I know these things now,
my slippers on the concrete, silent movements
in my memory, the sun setting in a re-enactment
of that moment's voluptuous logic.

Even now I can't see why they happen, these
sudden paroxysm in which everything is changed.
See only the landscapes that surround me now.
Each memory is like a grace sensorium. Each
landscape is an index by which I tick off little
ironies.

When I was a very small child these compulsions
began. Wound sleepless in sheets the views of my
short past would entangle with visions of the
future. There was a mud world. Men and women sought
to put together clear words of hope, to send them
surging like a river.

If you open the door to these visions the river
gives you no chance. Swept along you snatch
glimpses of your rolling, growing past. The current
does not cease. You fumble. You debate which stroke
to use. You are defenceless.

You take the words of hope, piece them one by one.
Making connections in mid-stream. Each of the fragments
is like a sickness that passes into you. When suddenly
you find yourself, hands and knees on sure ground, it
is only that the river has emptied itself.

You ask: was there a warning? Only in the memory. Only
when the mind's eye regards the drowned flame trees
and thorn trees which were buffeted by the roar of
terrible lives.

Ever since then, black in my heart, over-heated,
I had wanted to dream my way back into your world.
To make you feel a distant desire, to buckle the
Meaty underpinnings of your lives.

To tell you of something still ripening, of a river
larger and more violent than the last, whose
cataracts and rapids, swirls of white water, will
pound and pour upon your doors and terraces and,
exaltingly, turn your futures deliquescent.

The Buddha said there are eight paths to the Way.
Each path is a process, right and inescapable.
On your terrace, mud-spattered, full of history,
eyes and hair wild, I am the low prophet of the
ninth path of warning.

My father knows I am returning. He feels the dampness
of my breath. From the same spot he views the fierce
beauty of the sunsets. All the family is waiting.
When the door flies open someone will be fumbling to

tell you what has happened. The torrent of words
trying compulsively to re-enact faithfully the gestures,
intricacies and doomed rituals of a mud world. The past
and future spluttering on your doorstep.

NOTES

1. Stephen Chan, https://www.theguardian.com/commentisfree/2009/dec/03/commonwealth-trinidad-tobago.

2. Edward W. Said, *On Late Style*, London: Bloomsbury, 2006.

3. For example, on Ricoeur: Stephen Chan, "A Problem for IR: How Shall We Narrate the Saga of the Bestial Man?" *Global Society*, 17:4, 2003.

4. From my collection, *Crimson Rain*, Lampeter: Mellen, 1991, pp 25–29.

5. Then the most notorious road in central Nairobi, famed for its armed robberies of tourists. As a dare I would walk up and down River Road, betting to my friends that no one would dare touch me. The Kung Fu films in the Casino Cinema at one end of River Road certainly helped.

6. This refers to the 1982 Israeli invasion of Lebanon and the siege of Palestinian headquarters in Beirut, intent upon driving the Palestinian Liberation Organization out of the region. Volunteers came to fight—to no avail. The PLO were exiled to Tunis. Colonel Berger was Malraux's fighting name in the French resistance but, before World War II, he had fought with the international brigades in Spain.

7. None of these consumer items were available in Lusaka. The magazines at least were perfect lightweight presents for friends back home. The Won Ton was the treat for myself.

8. Brother Francis Omondi of the Marianist Brothers. These Catholic Brothers somehow discovered me and adopted me and for two years prayed each day at Matins for my soul. Nicknamed Omo, after the washing powder—he washed souls whiter than snow—he took me on the nightly feeding missions of the parking boys—so called because they hustled to look after parked cars for a tip. As a result of the mid-night feeding runs I was able to demonstrate to the Ministry of Social Development that its analysis of the parking boys as a discrete "problem" was a mythology. They were parts of entire families on the streets.

9. This means what it says. I understood why medieval priests indulged in flagel-lation. It is in fact an indulgence. A public effort to relieve the burden of guilt. In this case that such a slum should exist. Basically, there is a martial arts practice based on a ritualised movement called Sanchin, where you can be whipped without pain or marks. It's harder than it looks. I would buy crates of beer and soft drinks and host parties for the community workers and elders. Omo wanted me to learn a lesson. I'm not sure what lesson he had in mind. Perhaps simply, "never forget."

10. The Kimani Court was my preferred hotel. Basically, all trip I had premonitions of what did occur. A military uprising against the government that failed, with the university students celebrating too soon, with the result that hundreds of them were shot dead. We received the news in the Mountains of the Moon in Uganda, trying to

decipher what had happened from the radio static. But when, finally, I returned to Nairobi to transit to Lusaka, red-beret Israeli-trained special forces had an iron grip on the airport. The siege of Beirut, in the meantime, had resulted in the slaughters in the Palestinian refugee camps of Sabra and Shatila by Israeli-affiliated militias.

11. From my collection, *Crimson Rain*, pp 60–62.

Index

Zuma, Jacob, 42

www.ingramcontent.com/pod-product-compliance
Lightning Source LLC
Chambersburg PA
CBHW021821270326
41932CB00007B/278